How It Feels to Be Black in the USA

Critical Storytelling

Series Editors

Nicholas D. Hartlep (*Berea College, Kentucky, USA*)
Brandon O. Hensley (*Wayne State University, Michigan, USA*)

Editorial Board

René Antrop-González (*State University of New York at New Paltz, New York, USA*)
Noelle W. Arnold (*Ohio State University, Ohio, USA*)
Daisy Ball (*Roanoke College, Virginia, USA*)
T. Jameson Brewer (*University of North Georgia, Georgia, USA*)
Cleveland Hayes (*Indiana University–Purdue University, Indianapolis, USA*)
Mohamed Nur-Awaleh (*Illinois State University, Illinois, USA*)
Valerie Pang (*San Diego State University, California, USA*)
Ligia Pelosi (*Victoria University, Australia*)
David Pérez II (*Syracuse University, New York, USA*)
Peggy Shannon-Baker (*Georgia Southern University, Georgia, USA*)
Christine Sleeter (*California State University, California, USA*)
Suzanne SooHoo (*Chapman University, California, USA*)
Mark Vicars (*Victoria University, Australia*)

VOLUME 9

The titles published in this series are listed at *brill.com/csto*

How It Feels to Be Black in the USA

Poetic Narratives for Racial Equity, Equality, Healing, and Freedom

By

Pierre W. Orelus

BRILL

LEIDEN | BOSTON

All chapters in this book have undergone peer review.

The Library of Congress Cataloging-in-Publication Data is available online at https://catalog.loc.gov

Typeface for the Latin, Greek, and Cyrillic scripts: "Brill". See and download: brill.com/brill-typeface.

ISSN 2590-0099
ISBN 978-90-04-52544-3 (paperback)
ISBN 978-90-04-52545-0 (hardback)
ISBN 978-90-04-52546-7 (e-book)

Copyright 2022 by Pierre W. Orelus. Published by Koninklijke Brill NV, Leiden, The Netherlands.
Koninklijke Brill NV incorporates the imprints Brill, Brill Nijhoff, Brill Hotei, Brill Schöningh, Brill Fink, Brill mentis, Vandenhoeck & Ruprecht, Böhlau and V&R unipress.
Koninklijke Brill NV reserves the right to protect this publication against unauthorized use. Requests for re-use and/or translations must be addressed to Koninklijke Brill NV via brill.com or copyright.com.

This book is printed on acid-free paper and produced in a sustainable manner.

To the memory of both George Floyd, who was murdered on May 26th, 2020 by four police officers, and the 10 Black people who were cowardly killed at a Tops Friendly Markets Store located in Buffalo, New York, on May 14th, 2022 by an 18 years old white supremacist. May their blood spark a peaceful revolution leading to systemic change!

∴

Contents

Foreword: How Does It Feel Like to Be a Problem in the United States of America?   XI
    Awad Ibrahim

Introduction   1

PART 1
Rethinking Blackness in the Colonial, Capitalist, and White Imperialist Americas

1   Feeling the Blues in the United States of America   9

2   In Search of a Safe Place   11

3   We're Not Going Anywhere   13

4   From the Ghetto to the Ivory Tower   14

5   The Resilient Black Woman   16

6   The Oppressed of the Americas   17

7   Feeling in Exile in My Own Land   19

8   The Misrepresentation of People of the Global Majority   20

9   The Vetted Immigrants   23

10   Phobias in the United States   25

11   The Narcissist with the Blue Eyes   26

12   Why Are Black People So Angry?   28

13   What Happens to the Black Nation?   30

14	Black Pride	33
15	The Woman Who Floats	35
16	Still Standing in Front of You	38
17	In Memory of George Floyd	40
18	How It Feels to Be Black in the Americas	42
19	We're Rising up in Multi Colors	44
20	Love Always Trumps over Hate	45
21	I Am Black, and I Am Enough!	46
22	How Real Love Feels Like	47
23	The COVID-19 Pandemic of Color	49
24	Love Is All That We Need	50
25	Raising Queer Teens	52
26	Cancer Sucks!	54
27	The Death of the Nation	55
28	When Love Is Gone	56
29	The Fear of Death	57
30	How to Spot a Psychopath	58
31	You're a Beautiful Wave	60
32	On Co-Parenting	62
33	The Depressed	63

CONTENTS

34 Discovering African Spirituality   65

35 On Forgiveness   66

36 Living in the Future   67

37 In Honor of Our Black Ancestors   68

38 The Beauty in Solitude   69

PART 2
Black Beauty, Love, and Healing

39 Where Is the God for Black People?   73

40 Black Exodus   75

41 Open Letter to Our Ancestors   77

42 Only the Truth Will Set us Free   78

43 Involuntary Exile   80

44 The Day of Revolt   82

45 Bloody Day   83

46 God, Where Are You?   84

47 The Black Child   85

48 Dear Black Women   86

49 African Goddess   88

50 Life as a Circle   89

51 Black Youth   90

52	I Have Another Dream 91
53	Light in Hope 92
54	Fighting for Humanity 93
55	Dark Night in the Heart of a Coup 94
56	The Danger of Words 95
57	You Are My Redemption 96
58	Dear White Americans: An Open Letter 97

Afterword: A Long and Immense Cry That Rips the Air!   102
Gina Thésée

FOREWORD

How Does It Feel Like to Be a Problem in the United States of America?

We are all poets. Yes, you read it correctly: you, I, and all of us are poets. By virtue of being human, we are brought into this world not by choice and we are condemned not only to improvise but write the story that is our life. Whether we are aware of it or not, we are the author of that story. We are put onto the stage of life with no script and no specific directions, so we must decide for ourselves how to live our lives and which directions we choose to go or take. We mostly live, give birth, and die. There is nothing really remarkable or eventful about our lives. That story becomes just another story, another verse in the poetry of life.

However, once in a while someone comes in with strong conviction, clear mind, convincing articulation, and incredible command for language to write a totally fresh verse. They are so eloquent in their language, so visionary in their conviction that the familiar, the immediate, and the known become unfamiliar and unknown. Richard Rotry (1989) calls them "strong poets." These are people who are horrified of simply being "a copy or a replica"; they have the courage and audacity to engage, look for, and think through the "blind impresses," the gaps and the blind spots of thoughts, ideas and practices. The blind impresses are the difficult knowledges—problems, if you like—that society prefers not to face, be it (micro-)aggression, blatant racism, war, xenophobia, homophobia or ethno-supremacy. In the face of formidable pressure, the strong poets will choose to walk through these "problems," so to speak, and deal with them at the individual, national and global level.

Some of this strong poetry is in Pierre Orelus's *How It Feels to Be Black in the USA*. We move between the purely poetic and the purely political in a compelling way. Indeed, the two are inseparable in this book of poetry. It calls on African ancestors not only for inspiration but as the foundation of humanity. In *How It Feels to Be Black in the USA*, a space of *métissage* is created where Diasporic Africans meet, where America (i.e. U.S.) meets immigration, phobias, narcissism, Black pride, Black rage, queerness, COVID-19, parenting, truth, exile, humanity, hope, and love. Before it does so, however, it has to haunt itself with what happened to George Floyd: How and why did that murder happen? Unless we deal with the question of George Floyd not as an event but as a manifestation of something deeper and systemic, the answer to Orelus's question, *How It Feels to Be Black in the USA*, can only can be: a problem. So, appropriately, this book of poetry should have been called: "How It Feels to Be a Problem in the USA?" Here, George Floyd's murder is a manifestation of the ugly cartography of anti-Black racism which has its deep roots and routes in history of racism, oppression, and systemic socio-racial and economic discrimination. Until we reach that point of consciousness, we have to poetically shout it out loud: Black Lives (Do) Matter!

Reference

Rorty, R. (1989). *Contingency, irony, and solidarity*. Cambridge University Press.

Awad Ibrahim
University of Ottawa

Introduction

I begin this introduction with a personal anecdote, as I strongly feel that story matters. While working on the introduction of this book, a very short video lasting about 30 seconds was sent to me via phone. Such video portrayed a white toddler who seemed scared of a black shadow that kept following her. Upon seeing such shadow, she cried inconsolably. As this innocent child was frantically running away from the black shadow reflected through the radiation of the sun, she eventually fell down showing a sad look on her face. Apparently, this video was intended to make the targeted recipient laugh. However, in critically examining it through a racial lens, I was able to draw the conclusions that follow.

I argue that the content of the video can be interpreted as the manifestation of racial fear and paranoia that many Whites experience when they see a black person walking in the street or, worse yet, in their neighborhood. Such fear and paranoia, which usually lead to what is commonly called *White fly*, are fueled by white supremacist ideology shaping the racially prejudiced mind, behavior, and actions of many people. White supremacist ideology has spread fear about people of color, whom many Whites are conditioned psychologically to running away from upon seeing their shadow. For example, in the mental universe of this innocent White child noted earlier, the shadow of Blacks is terrifying, let alone their physical presence.

While talking to a colleague of mine about the video, he mentioned the massacre occurring in Charleston, South Carolina, USA, on the evening of June 17th, 2015 leading to the terrible loss of nine precious African American lives. The conclusion that he and I drew from this horrible tragedy was that, like the nine harmless African Americans who were cruelly massacred by Dyllan Roof while they were praying and singing in a church, any person of African descent could have been the victim of this white supremacist and terrorist act, for there is no safe zone for Black and Brown people in in the United States of America. Neither highly educated nor formally un-educated people of color, neither the rich nor the poor, neither the straight nor the queer, and, finally, neither the conservative nor the progressive is exempt of institutional racism and white supremacy in this country.

Like the 10 Black people who were cowardly killed at a Tops Friendly Markets Store located in Buffalo, New York, on May 14th, 2022 by a teen white supremacist, the African Americans alluded above were bloodily murdered at the church as if their lives did not matter at all. In the eyes of their KKK murderers, they were just sub-humans representing a threat to the white race and, therefore, must be disappeared on the face of the planet wherein only Whites are worth inhabiting. In their delusionary, white supremacist mindset, that's the only truth there is—a criminally type of racist truth whereby they might have been infected at home, in schools, in churches, and from the mainstream media. They acted on such truth, which perhaps has been sold to them since childhood.

White supremacist ideology practices lead to terrorist acts, like that of Dyllan. White supremacist ideology knows neither doors nor gates. It infiltrates people's places and the minds of people far deeper than one realizes. In the mind of a white supremacist person, Black and Brown people are savage, violent, untrustworthy, stupid, and lazy individuals that must be wiped out of the planet for the safety and survival of the White race. This is to say that White supremacists, as this book points out, do not exempt any Black or Brown person from their targets, irrespective of their light skin privileges or social status. All Black and Brown people have been victims of police harassment and brutality, micro-aggression, and institutional racism. Their days are numbered in White America. Black and brown people are constantly subjected to white KKK violence—psychological, symbolic, physical or otherwise. There is no protected zone for Black and Brown people—not even at home, in churches or in schools.

They are constantly under the gaze of white supremacy and KKK terrorism. People of color are not protected under the law like everybody else; they are treated as second-class citizens even though many of them are high achievers and accomplished citizens who have contributed to the prosperity of the United States. White supremacist ideologies and practices are responsible for the psychological, emotional, and material sufferings of Black and Brown men and women. Black and brown lives, including transgenders', do not matter in the eyes of many people. The senseless, inhumane, and unlawful killings of Black and Brown people by police officers are prime examples. These killings have made people of color fear for their lives.

While being brutalized and murdered by police officers and racist Whites, people of color continue to be lectured by politicians and well-paid media pundits on American exceptionalism, including American ideals of democracy, freedom, and human rights. We have also been lectured on the so-called post-racial era, even though attacks on the body of Black and Brown people, their human dignity, freedom, and sacred lives have been intensified every year. In addition, Black and Brown soldiers have been injured and killed overseas in wars defending imperialist interests of oligarch individuals and groups in this country—all in the name of western democracy and freedom at home and abroad. Yet, when they return home, they receive ill treatment from their country whose geopolitical interests they served and defended overseas. Their mistreatment includes being racially and economically marginalized in addition to experiencing mental health issues.

Why Write This Book?

Since the dawn of time, poetry and stories, which I call here poetic narratives, have been used to address social issues while inspiring at the same time deep, imaginary, and philosophical thoughts. This book aims to achieve similar goals. Specifically, this book combines poetry with short stories situated in very specific historical, racial, socio-economic, and cultural contexts to examine the existential experiences of Brown and Black people in the Americas, particularly in the United States of America, with systemic racism, white supremacy, voucher capitalism, xenophobia, and sexism, among other social wrongs. This book goes on to illuminate the manner in which these systemic forms of oppression have affected them psychologically, academically, and materially.

As I was working on this book, I felt, and continue to feel, deeply sad learning about the murder of George Floyd. On June 1st, 2020, approximately a week ago after George Floyd was murdered, I was talking to a former Black police officer about his murder while taking a walk. The former officer and I focused the whole conversation on the lack of safety experiencing Black and Brown people in the United States of America.

As we were talking about it, we started to release our anger over the phone. At some point during the conversation, I forgot about my surroundings, including some White people who were walking behind me. I was so angry about George's murder that I did not care who was listening to what I was saying. The former police officer, who is an acquaintance, suddenly interjected and stated, "Any Black person could have been George, even myself, a former police officer who received the same training as these officers who murdered him." Agreeing with him, I replied and said, "Yes, this could have been anyone, regardless of their status in society." I went on to add, "It does not matter if you are a professor or a lawyer because being Black in the United States of America simply means being in danger." I stopped suddenly speaking in the middle of the conversation as I felt that I was about to burst into tears.

My throat started to crack while my eyes were feeling heavier and red, and I was sweating much faster. Without him knowing perhaps, this former officer took some heaviness and anger away from me when he started shouting out "They are the same everywhere. It does not matter if it is here or in another country." I amplified what he said stating, "They are brutalizing and killing us everywhere, and that's not fair."

As the conversation progressed and brought to me both recent and old bad memories, I got angrier, and I wanted to cry but I held my anger and tears, as I did not want anyone to see me crying, particularly the White folks who were, too, taking their daily walk. Crying would have been the basic human and healing thing to do to release anger, but I felt embarrassed and was unsure how people on the street would perceive and interpret it. Some people would have probably asked if I was okay and offered help, while others would have walked by and gone on with their day.

Regardless of the possible scenario described above, I was, and I am still, angry about the murder of George Floyd and other Black and Brown people who have been killed since, including the ones murdered at a Tops Friendly Markets Store in Buffalo, New York, on May 14th, 2022. For example, When George Floyd was murdered, I was living in a mixed neighborhood called *Black Rock*, located in Bridgeport, Connecticut, sharing border with another city, Fairfield, which is predominantly White. Although many self-proclaimed White liberals lived there and seemed friendly, I never felt safe. The White folks walked their dogs peacefully every day, while I often got scared of the police car that always drove patrolling the whole area. At times, if felt as if the police who patrolled the rich neighborhood annexed to the place where I lived was keeping an eye on Black people. I always got scared as he purposely made the point that I saw him every time he drove by. I do not think it was a coincidence.

Although I enjoyed walking by an ocean situated next to some fancy houses, namely mansions, I detested seeing the same police office either driving by or standing on the corner to make himself visible. I wonder if Whites experienced the same feeling as I did when I saw him, or if they even paid attention to him at all. As for me, however, he was on my forehead, and so I kept an eye on him like he kept his eyes on me. As a Black man, I have been advised to avoid eye contact with police officers, so I never looked at him but I made sure I watched every single move he made. Sadly, we treated each other as though we shared a painful personal beef, although that was not the case.

Systemic racism has made Whites and non-Whites feel as if they're enemies who are at war with one another; they distrust one another. Because of my constant inner fear of police officers, I feel that I can't get loose with them. When a White police officer or a group of police officers are coming my way, I often feel that I am in danger, as I know that in their racially biased mind and eyes, I am just a bad guy that they can get off the street if they want to by abusing their power. It does not matter if I am a professor, a decent father and, above all, a family man with no criminal record. But these attributes do not matter to racist police officers other than my black skin tone.

These conclusions are drawn both on painful personal experiences with White police officers as well as the savage ways in which I have seen them treat other people of color, like George Floyd, Breonna Taylor, and Ahmaud Arbery, illustrating the manifestation of white supremacist ideology and practices. Such ideology makes Whites believe that, particularly White police officers, they can kill people of color without impunity. As a Black man, I have become increasingly very angry every time I talk about the killings of Black and Brown people by White police officers and racist individual Whites. I can't even keep up with number of Black and Brown men whose lives were shattered in the bloody hands of racist Whites.

I have sought therapy as an alternative to cope with deep anger these social wrongs have caused me, and it has helped. However, as I have reflected on my own experience as a Black man in the Americas and that of other people of color who are facing daily racial oppression, I ask whether we need therapy to cope with the racist system that has made Black and Brown people sick, both mentally and physically, or a revolution to eradicate it, particularly as people of color are routinely murdered.

Is it fair that Black and Brown people have to seek therapy and other forms of coping mechanism to cope with systemic racism? Likewise, is it just to expect other marginalized groups, including abused women and the LGBTQ people, to do the same because of sexism, patriarchy, and homophobia? Therapy, as I have come to personally experience and understand it, is not a permanent fix to any problem or trauma, rather a peaceful and healthier way to first cope with and hopefully heal from it, which can be a long process. I believe that the key is to work together to eradicate racism as well as voucher capitalism through structural policy changes. We need to let go of policies that have been serving mostly White males, particularly self-identified heterosexual and Christian White males.

What is more, we need to get rid of policies that include allocating much more resources to institutions, like the police force, which has been the biggest enemy of Black and Brown people, than education and health care, which are the motor of society. Finally, we need to change policies that allow police officers to brutalize and murder Blacks and other people of color without being held accountable. Nobody is above the law, so police officers should not be the exception. They have killed countless people of color and have gotten away with their murder. Where is the justice and liberty for all, as mentioned in the constitution of the United States of America?

Racist policies are inequitable and inhumane. Therefore, they reflect neither justice nor liberty for all. These policies must be changed, as they have allowed police officers and individual Whites to racially profile and kill people of color, who have been historically denied the benefit of their humanity. They are portrayed like animals, savages, criminals and thugs by many Whites, including the former American president, Donald J. Trump, who constantly used these words to refer to Black and Latinx people, including immigrants of color, during his presidential campaign and beyond.

Racism alongside with savage capitalism and toxic masculinity must continuously be exposed until they are eradicated, whether it be through creative writing, like poetry and narratives, and other forms of genre and peaceful means, including activism. This poetry book aims to contribute to achieving this noble goal. Specifically, it aims to unmask and help better understand the continued effects of systemic racism, white supremacy, xenophobia, voucher capitalism, and colonization on the oppressed of color, particularly those living in the United States of America.

PART 1

Rethinking Blackness in the Colonial, Capitalist, and White Imperialist Americas

∴

CHAPTER 1

Feeling the Blues in the United States of America

They take over our land, then seize power to keep us oppressed and colonized.
They need our labor but call us savages who have to be controlled and scrutinized.
They illegally place us in jails, where we are treated as strangers and mere objects.
Spying and water boarding techniques have been their favorite political subjects.

They label immigrants of color, particularly Muslims, as dangerous, domestic terrorists,
When all they have wanted to do is to come to America to work, study or visit as tourists.
They have tried to silence the voice of the oppressed so that the latter would not resist or fight.
But the oppressed are determined even though they have been targeted daily and at night.

Since corporations took over the land, the oppressed have been earning minimum wage.
Indeed, the oppressed of all colors have been exploited regardless of their gender and age.
They go on strike fighting against the system but they are brutalized by police officers,
Who unfairly punish them for standing against voucher capitalists who are indeed robbers.

The oppressed have been offered loans for which they are not all qualified.
Many have unexpectedly faced foreclosure, and they are terribly terrified.
Yet they are criticized for making a decision that was supposedly reckless.
While corporate banks are bailed out, the oppressed have become homeless.

Oppressed of color have been treated in this society as if they were newly enslaved.
Fortunately, they are constructors of their liberation path, which must now be paved.
For this collective project, the oppressed are ready to die until the victorious day,
Knowing there will be obstacles, including setbacks causing unexpected delay.

CHAPTER 2

In Search of a Safe Place

Doesn't matter if you are light or dark skin,
For you are always in danger, everywhere,
Even though you have both your arms and feet.
You do not commit any crime or harm anyone,
You're still murdered everywhere from the tree to the street.
Whether black or brown, your body is damped in trashes,
While your blood is running through the Mississippi river.
A cruel racist act, supported by racist Whites,
That you just can't bear.

You're walking in the park peacefully during the day in bright light,
And they see you as a threat, and few hours later you are killed.
You're jogging peacefully in broad day light in your neighborhood,
And you're suddenly followed and killed by two Whites, father and son.
Isn't it a malicious, racist act that deserves legal accountability?

You're accused of stealing in a store by a person of color.
You're then followed by four White male officers on duty.
You're at their mercy; one of them put his knees on your neck
While you beg for your life saying to them, please let me go, "sir."
One of them proceeds to suffocate you anyway despite your plea,
For he does not see your humanity in theirs because of their racist mind.

The black teen entered a neighborhood patrolled
By a self-declared community eye watcher.
He was shot dead while he tried to defend himself.
But the media tried to cover up the truth about this murder case.

A beautiful soul and smart nursing student,
Who was in her bed sleeping with her boyfriend.
And cops broke into her house and started shooting.
And she was dead while the boyfriend barely survived.

A Black boy was playing in the park with a toy and he was shot dead.
While a grown Black man was selling cigarettes in the street of New York to survive,
The police came and strangled him while supposedly trying to arrest him.
He said "I can't breathe," but they ignored his desperate cry for his life,
Which was cowardly vanished few hours later while laying down in a hospital bed.

A handicapped young Black man was in a wheelchair when they still brutally beat him up,
And he later died, but no police officer is behind bars paying for their unlawful action.
This young man did not commit any crime, but he was portrayed as a danger.
Everything that has been constructed about Blacks is presented as a danger,
And they have been treated harshly as a result in the United States of America,
A country, where there is neither compassion nor love for people of color.

CHAPTER 3

We're Not Going Anywhere

We are portrayed as a real danger in the media, including in Hollywood movies.
But we are not going anywhere; we are here to stay in the USA or Europe,
Even when we are racially profiled, arrested, beaten, handcuffed, and jailed,
And even if we are perceived as Ms. danger, Mr. danger or simply danger.

We are not going anywhere from our native land you shamelessly stole.
It is now terribly deteriorated, and it does not seem like you care.
We're not asking you to go back to Europe, your original place;
Why do you ask us to go back to Africa or simply to our country?

Do not call us nigger, and we will not call you White supremacist or racist.
Do not call us violent because you're insulting your White ancestors,
Who were colonizers invading, raping, and murdering innocent people of color.
Do not call us rapist because your White colonialists are the pioneers par excellence.

We are the danger you have created for centuries, and it is now spilled on your face.
We are what you will never know with your blind racial prejudice and hypocrisy.
We are the descendant of kings, queens, scientists, chiefs, inventors, and artists.
We are everything in every human; we're the bridge of the world you always cross!

CHAPTER 4

From the Ghetto to the Ivory Tower

John's parents did not own much, and they did not go far in school.
Growing up, John had no access to safe water. And that was not cool.
In schools, teachers had low expectation of him because of his non-standard English.
They did not treat him the same way as they treated his classmates who were Irish.

Because of his distinct way of speaking English, sometimes he felt visible,
But most of the time, in the eyes of many of his peers, he was not all noticeable.
He has been discriminated against for his Ebonics perceived as a working-class accent.
In schools, only linguistically sensitive teachers supported him one hundred percent.

After he finished graduate school, he was hired as a professor after a rigorous search.
He was very happy after spending many years teaching and doing empirical research.
But he is realizing that in the academy, alone, he can't really effect systemic change.
He has been told that his rebellious ideas will not serve him, but he has refused to change.

They call him a radical for challenging students to think critically so they can act otherwise.
Some of his colleagues have repeatedly told him that risking his career doing so is not wise.
Students have reported him to his superior for his radical political views and positions.
He has been punished for criticizing people and government married with corporations.

Some students whose privileges he questions state that he is a crazy preacher.
They often complain to the dean that he is a radical and a socialist teacher.
He has been called in to explain his teaching method and ideological position.
Fortunately, this form of surveillance has been now denounced across the nation.

CHAPTER 5

The Resilient Black Woman

Because of her dark skin and size, she is often unfairly targeted and poorly treated.
When the police killed her father, her mother and other siblings really felt decimated.
She became angry with a legal system that protected a murder who killed her father.
She felt then, and still feels, that this system does not like Black people to go farther.

After her father died, her mother became an addict and died of a massive heart attack.
She did not expect this, especially right after she, alongside her siblings, had a snack.
Since her parents' death, she has been feeling lost and doubtful about her future.
Her father's murder has caused her sorrow, deep mental disturbance and rupture.

Her mother was denied health coverage for her addiction, and she, as result, died.
Her health insurance refused to pay for her mother's surgery, and she bitterly cried.
But she knew crying would not bring her back, so she fought very hard for justice.
She organized a protest but was again brutalized in the street by the racist police.

She was forced to live in unsafe neighborhoods and was often thrown in jail.
Fighting with inmates and working for cheap labor in prison felt really like hell.
After she was released, she fell into deep alcoholism to cope with her chronic depression.
She overcame it but was still judged in a country where they talk a lot about human compassion.

CHAPTER 6

The Oppressed of the Americas

Poor children swim in a dirty river poisoning the water running through a town.
That river is full of chemical waste coming from factories that were shut down.
The CEOs of these factories maximized their profits and left shamelessly.
Meanwhile, people in the neighborhood have been losing their lives daily.

The oppressed have witnessed their houses being destroyed by bombs from an occupying army.
The oppressed have been murdered. During the 50s, they were called communists, the enemy.
As a result, they were forced to live in a refugee camp for almost a quarter of a century.
While living in this camp, they suffered severe emotional distress and psychological injury.

They live under an oppressive government and experience many forms of violence.
They lost family members in wars and witnessed many of them losing their sense.
They have become disenchanted in this land destroyed by deep racial divide.
And they see those in power as people who have never been on their side.

The oppressed of the Americas have been forced to flee from the so-called democratic land.
They have been facing war and racial discrimination, and no one wants to give them a hand.
Those in power have insulted, stepped on, and purposely misrepresented their religion.
They are targeted every day, as a result, by those who do not share the same religion.

In their native land, they faced poverty, civil war, genocide, colorism, and sexism.
In the land of the free, they face institutional racism, xenophobia, and linguicism.
Their race, ethnicity, sexuality, and religion have made them become an easy target.
They have been profiled, which really feels like being hit by a psychological bullet.

Upon returning home from wars abroad, oppressed soldiers went to a restaurant to buy food.
It was on a very sunny day, so they were happy and felt genuinely in a very good mood.
They entered the restaurant and were ignored. For hours, they were not asked to be seated.
Suddenly, a white person came, and he was immediately served. They felt deeply defeated.

The oppressed went to wars fighting for America and returned home psychologically damaged.
They lost their legs and arms for a country that doesn't give a dam. So, they deeply feel enraged.
The government has lied to them and failed to provide them with adequate mental healthcare.
They have been asking: what has happened to our years of service? And nobody seems to care.

CHAPTER 7

Feeling in Exile in My Own Land

I have been feeling in exile in my own land because of my ideology.
I have been in exile because I stand up against all sorts of demagogy.
I think differently, and for that I have been attacked by the powerful.
In their eyes, I am nothing but a lost case, a looser, or simply just a fool.

I feel in exile in my own land because of its long history of imperialism and colonization.
I voice my feelings but nobody wants to listen, as they want to avoid possible confrontation.
I will continue speaking up until I feel that I am treated with dignity as a living human being. Regardless of prejudices, I will step forward with love and respect as the best way of being.

I will stop feeling in exile when my race, religion, and culture are respected.
I will feel that I am part of the mainland when I am no longer racially targeted.
And when I am no longer called a traitor for speaking against social injustice.
And when historically marginalized groups can finally see the light of justice.

Black and Brown Americans have been feeling in exile in their own land,
Which many people around the world have fanatically called a democratic land.
I would be most proud of this land if these fat lies were not circulated in school.
Racially biased History teachers have fed students these lies, and that is not cool.

CHAPTER 8

The Misrepresentation of People of the Global Majority

You say that if we decide to go on strike, you can break all of us,
In small pieces, because you were the ones who enchained us.
With arrogance, you said that we, people of color, should have all realized,
By now, that our forcibly captured African ancestors were not civilized,
That they lived in caves, and that they were uneducated, stupid, and savage,
Like untamed animals that must be placed in their place in a tied cage.

You say that we're physically strong, and we look scary because we're Black.
Is it why you want to stand on our neck, break it, and refuse to fix it back?
Sometimes, you look at our skin and call us names like yellow or brown,
And then you say, if we behave well and remain silent, we can stick around.
You even have the nerve to say that our hair is kinky and very nappy,
That we should straighten it to make it look white, if we want to be happy.

You have portrayed us in the media as violent and lazy.
When we make our voice heard, you say that we're crazy.
You saw some of us walking fast in the school hallway,
And without thinking, you abruptly interrupted us and asked:
Are you the new housekeeper, the coach, or the new Janitor?
You do not even think for a moment that one of us can be a professor.

You say that our nose is too big, too flat, or simply looks too African.
That to look and feel good, we must have one that looks European.
You say that we eat too much, and that we're too big and too fat.
And that to look attractive and sexy, our belly has to be really flat.

In the 80s, you stated that we caught the Aids Virus because we were careless.
And you later accused us of caching the COVID-19 virus because were reckless.

With regard to our racial identity, you have tried to distort everything,
For your racist goal is to misrepresent us as if I we were nothing.
You say that we're a rebel for refusing to follow your European standard.
As a severe punishment, you say that we will always be under your radar.
But you refuse to challenge your heterosexual and white male unearned privilege.
And you deny your homophobic, racist, and sexist behavior, despite your age.

As we're walking on the street, you look at us and say: what a sexy and fresh meat!
Your friends laugh, laugh, and laugh again, and you say that's cool, that's very neat.
The next day you see us; you look at us and say to your friends: Isn't she exotic?
We ignore you, but you keep staring at us and then ask: Are you an Asiatic?
In your blue eyes, we're nothing but a thing to play with, a sexual object,
Which you arrogantly feel you can use, reuse, and, if so desire, reject.

You blame us for our misery, poverty, and victimization,
As if we were the ones who created our own dire condition.
You put us in jail unjustly so that you can exploit us and wrongly take away our breath,
Which we need so we can be physically here for our family on this polluted earth.

You say that our culture is barbarous and very inferior,
While you sell yours as well-advanced and by far superior.
When we speak up against racial, sexual, and socio-economic inequalities,
You say that we're losing all of our senses fighting against inequities.
And when we stand up for those who are marginalized and hungry,
You look at us and say: why are you, people of color, so angry?

You can't tolerate our skin and accent, so you say: go back to your native land,
Instead of distributing the resources you stole and kept in your bloody western hand.
We fight back saying: our land was colonized and has been brutally exploited.
It's still a poor land that you imperialist and neo-colonizers have still manipulated.
When we dare call you on your racial prejudice, you look at us as if we were a big mess.
You ignore us, looking down on our cultural heritage and criticizing how we dress.

In your textbooks, you have lied completely about our history,
Which you have put under siege for more than a century.
You have used all kinds of tricks to belittle our humanity,
Which has been attacked and infected by your cruelty.
Then you accuse us of committing too much crime and of being too violent.
But you do not mind at all enjoying our folk music and exploiting our talent.

And you still say: why are we so poor? Why can't we go to a good school and get a job?
And you rush to conclude that we don't want to work because we just want to rob.
You have monopolized most of the earth resources: isn't that really greedy and racist?
We would not be poor if racism and capitalism, which have been your tool, did not exist.

CHAPTER 9

The Vetted Immigrants

On countless occasions neighbors have reported them both to the police and the FBI.
FBI agents have broken in their houses to search for dangerous weapons with an evil eye.
They have been called all kind of names, like terrorists, dirty thugs, and drug traffickers.
They have been wrongly detained, for their religion and skin color are seen social markers.

They work in fields picking up strawberries, apples, oranges, blueberries, and tomatoes.
Chemicals used to grow these crops have affected their whole body, including their toes.
Yet xenophobic and racist politicians have called them illegal immigrants and rapists.
These empty speeches are empty of compassion, and these politicians need therapists.

The vetted have been searched at airports because of their nationality and physical appearance.
They have been detained for challenging authorities about their lack of acceptance.
The government has threatened to deport them despite their American citizenship.
They have been treated as if they were dumped here like African slaves in a big ship.

Jose's car was dropped dead while driving, and he needed to get to the grocery.
He called some friends and asked them for a ride. One of them picked him up in his mercury.
When they got to the super market, the cashier literally treated Jose as if he was nothing.
Meanwhile, Whites paid for their grocery calmly and did not have to worry about anything.

© PIERRE W. ORELUS, 2022 | DOI:10.1163/9789004525467_010

Jose's best friend and two members of his family died crossing the border.
The coyote blamed them for their death; they failed to carefully follow his order.
One died of dehydration while the other was shot by an American border patrol.
Jose has been mourning their death and, at times, feels that he is about to lose control.

Four of his family members and two of his co-workers were unexpectedly deported.
Children left behind have been asking why their parents have been so mistreated.
FBI agents have come to Jose's house searching for the "illegal," the undocumented.
They have harassed his parents and his little brother, and he has felt really tormented.

Many Americans have been taken for Muslims because they look Arab or speak fluent Arabic.
They have sometimes made them feel as if they pose a danger to the so-called great republic.
Police officers have searched their cars many times asking them Islamophobic question:
"Do you happen to know Muhamed? We would sincerely appreciate your corporation."

Muhamed's best friend disappeared and found dead near an abandoned car.
A note was left saying: dirty Terrorist! His death has caused him a very deep scar.
His murderer was never identified and no one knows when, if ever, he will be found.
Many Muslims are scared walking in the street alone, and their fear is real and profound.

CHAPTER 10

Phobias in the United States

A Muslim student was harassed by a man for being suspected to be "illegal" and gay.
His male homophobic aggressor asked those who challenged him if they were, too, gay.
He was told no, and was asked: does a man need to be gay in order to defend gays' right?
The aggressor ignored the question, and said instead: "I hope I was clear," as if he got it right.

In the US, immigrants of color have experienced the effects of structural racism and xenophobia.
But Muslims in particular have been visibly subjected to systemic racism and islamophobia.
These experiences have shaped political awakening and forged their consciousness,
With which they, as a people, need to continue to live while facing daily inhumane mess.

CHAPTER 11

The Narcissist with the Blue Eyes

He is materially rich, yet spiritually poor and emotionally empty to govern a nation.
He shows, through his blatant racist, xenophobic, misogynist, and sexist action,
A heart full of rage, hatred and insecurity leading to deep mental imbalance,
Which seems to have deeply aggravated his fragile ego since his adolescence.

He finds joy in self-contemplation, repeated self-admiration and self-promotion.
He attracts conservatives and racists with similar type of contagious fascist passion,
Which he shows through self-importance that blinds him, let alone his constant self-praise.
He promotes himself as the best entrepreneur who gives himself a humble annual raise.

He has internalized and acted upon racist, fascist, and white supremacist ideology,
Surfaced in his authoritarian, self-serving behavior and actions without any apology.
He feeds his ego from psychological violence that he causes to his perceived enemies.
His abusive actions are shown through his self-righteous and justified controversies.

He is extravagant, and has an intimidating voice and attitude toward journalists,
Who are not intimidated by his rant saying that they are not real nationalists.
He conspires against those who challenge him or he perceives as a barrier.
He misleads people with his male empty rhetoric on business sans frontier,

Which he does preach in his daily interaction with people, including business men,
From whom he craves for attention and with whom he shares the club of rich men.
He always wants to be right; he gets defensive when he is challenged in public.
His male ego is very fragile, and is very insecure and weak to lead the republic.

He is oppressive, condescending, and a public performer with no substance.
He seems value performance over substance and appearance over essence.
He wants people to embrace his world and feed his ego at any price.
He is a mediocre who has used people to get ahead, and that's not nice.

He promotes those who bow to him, including colonized Black and Brown brothers,
While demonizing those who stand up to him, including some of our elected sisters,
Who provide a message of respect, change and solidarity with the Black or Brown,
Who are devasted by systemic racism that deeply hurts and puts millions of them down.

CHAPTER 12

Why Are Black People So Angry?

This question is loaded with both explicit and implicit racial biases,
And it is often damped on Black and Brown people countless times.
The real question that ought to be asked: Why aren't you, too, angry?
Perhaps, you're not angry because you are not subject to police killings.
Maybe, you're not angry because of your white privileges.
Of course, you're not angry because you do not have to deal with racism and white supremacy.
How can you be angry when you have never been called dirty animals, thugs, and criminals?
Well, you're not angry because your race is not seen as a threat to the western world.
Maybe, you're not angry because you're not racially profiled everywhere you happen to be.
Would not you be angry if you were constantly racially profiled and daily harassed?
Would not you display anger if you were unfairly labeled as violent and dirty immigrants?
Would you not be angry if your self-confidence was often mistaken for being arrogant?
Would not you be angry if you were looked down upon because of your skin color?
Would not you be angry if you were not taken seriously because of your ethnicity?
Would not you be angry if you were called savage because you're Black or Brown?
Would not you be angry if you were constantly labeled and portrayed as gangster, savage?
You're not angry because of your white privileges, which you take for granted.
You're not angry because you are not forced to attend underfunded schools.
You're not angry because you are not forced to live in marginalized and unsafe neighborhoods.
You are not angry because they don't prohibit you from speaking your language in schools.

You're not angry because they do not look down on your speech pattern or accent.

You're not angry because your peers do not make fun of your name and physical appearance.

You're not angry because of your unearned privileges that your race has afforded you.

Would not you be angry if you were victims of all sorts of violence because of your skin?

CHAPTER 13

What Happens to the Black Nation?

What happens to the *Black Nation*?
where colonized and enslaved Africans successfully fought against
White oppressors and gained their independence and freedom,
where the school system, including the public-school system, was strong
and competitive with other school systems abroad,
and where the water was not contaminated with infectious diseases.

What happens to the *Black Nation*?
where farmers used to grow organic local food, which was accessible
and affordable;
where children were safe playing in public parks and on the street;
where the cost of living was low;
and where there was a deep sense of community shared by everyone.

What happens to the *Black Nation*?
where resilient and ordinary people often woke up early in the morning
to go to work, to go to the local market to sell and buy basic necessities;
where people felt safe at home;
and where people were free to circulate on the street late a night.

What happens to the *Black Nation*?
where people used to drink, dance, play dominoes, basketball, football
or soccer, talk about local politics without fighting one another with
dangerous weapons;
where people used to buy food from local street vendors and farmers;
and where ordinary folks laughed, played and listened to music in their
backyard or on the street.

What happens to the *Black Nation*?
where its inhabitants now do not have employments and are deprived
of access to quality education; where having access to basic literacy
skills is a luxury for millions of people;
where the school system is still operating among the debris of
colonialism;

and where the legal system is controlled by the powerful and functions mostly for them.

What happens to the *Black Nation*?
currently devastated by poverty and divisions among politicians obsessed with power, wealth, and fame;
where innocent people are killed on a daily basis by gangs;
where thousands of children are homeless and dying of hunger, malnutrition, and pollution
while large amounts of money are spent to buy weapons to kill and stay in power.

What happens to the *Black Nation*?
where the majority of its people have to struggle daily for a single meal, while a small privileged class is living a luxurious life;
where countless numbers of people, particularly children are dying of diarrhea and other curable diseases;
and where the majority of the people do not have access to quality food and the environment is constantly under attack.

What happens to the *Black Nation*?
where young women are the sexual objects of older rich men;
where young girls are sexually harassed, raped, and beaten by these men;
where being a man is defined as having three or more girls or women treated as subalterns.

What happens to the *Black Nation*?
where the wealthy or simply those with some form of economic capital treat domestic workers as modern house slaves;
where politicians and so-called leaders arm poor teenage boys as death squads to murder their opponents so as to stay in power;
and where human rights are a meaningless concept to those in power or simply those who are armed.

What happens to the *Black Nation*?
from which you hold your most cherished memories but which you hope to leave soon because of abject poverty, daily violence, and inequality;
because of grotesque abuse of human rights;

and because it is a place where simply speaking out against torture and governmental corruption is taken as a threat to the ruling class.

What happens to the *Black Nation*?
where you are fearful and feeling unsafe because your political stance against prostitution, which has become a way for survival for many young girls and women, both educated and uneducated;
where *Sugar daddy* practices, involving young and vulnerable women having paid sex with privileged older men, becomes common practice; and where women are overworked and underpaid in factories producing brand shoes like NIKE but can't feed themselves and their families.

CHAPTER 14

Black Pride

No, it is not insolence. Nor is it, like you often accuse of us, arrogance.
It is not anger either. It is Black pride full of dignity and confidence.
Perhaps you have never expected us to be assertive and confident,
So, you labeled us as being too cocky or simply overconfident.

We do not allow the legacy of slavery dictates how to be or simply how to talk,
So do not use this factor to judge the way we live our lives, behave or walk.
It is not our problem if you only read us through your white Eurocentric lenses,
Which have caused your prejudice aimed at making us lose our senses.

We know that during the era of slavery and colonization,
Our ancestors were not allowed to any form of freedom or assertion.
They were only expected to shut up and allow themselves to be oppressed.
They were prohibited from saying things that would make the masters feel stressed.

The atrocity occurring during slavery caused scar to many in the Black community.
A legal document was needed to protect their human rights, dignity, and sanity.
Hence, the declaration of human rights is a very important legal document.
Such a document was written during a monumental historical moment.

It was hoped that with this document Black and Brown Lives would be protected.
And that other minority groups and individuals would not be vetted and targeted.
But it is an illusion, as people of color's rights have been violated and stepped on.
We hold deep hope and resilience in our heart and soul that the struggle will go on.

Our ancestors were expected to be hard workers, extremely polite, and submissive.
Their children were also expected to be obedient, to work hard, and to be passive.
Our ancestors were real warriors who fought against their oppressors and won victories.
Despite their resilience and brilliance, however, they knew many forms of injuries.

In the racist mind, we are not expected to show a strong sense of self-empowerment.
Nor are we expected to challenge those in power despite their very ill treatment.
When we talk with confidence, they often see, read, and judge us as being arrogant.
As if, because we're the descendant of slaves, we are not expected to be confident.

A strong sense of self-affirmation is not expected of the descendant of the enslaved.
This is a historical fact that can't be denied, so it needs to be critically analyzed.
Many labels have been wrongly placed on Black and Brown identity.
This has been done repeatedly throughout centuries, and this is just insanity.

Yes, we, Black and Brown, are proud, and we are not afraid of asserting ourselves.
We're well-assured, and paranoia certainly does not absolve our soul, our inner selves.
Do not mistake our dignity and pride for arrogance and our passion for aggressiveness,
For our speech pattern reflects our culture and history, as our words reflect our assertiveness.

CHAPTER 15

The Woman Who Floats

She moves like a river with her irresistible intelligence and sparky smile.
She has an incredible ability to convince others with her intellect and style.
She behaves as if she owns all the places where she has been.
She lives up to that expectation liberating her whole self.
She takes firm positions based on her principles and values that define her womanhood,
She shows self-respect, respect, compassion, and love for humanity.
She moves around, in circle, forward and backward with strong legs.
Whether she moves fast or goes at a slow pace, she walks with personality and confidence.
She smiles with her heart and soul, while dancing with passion in an infectious way.
She seems possessed when she dances, and she speaks with passionate oratory moves.
She is multicolor in her discourse, passion, moves, heart, soul, and beauty.
She fully masters the art of speaking; she speaks like an intellectual without border.
She is often portrayed in the media as a sexually exotic, superficial, and out of control,
When all she has been trying to do is to enjoy life in its full moon while on this earth.
She is seen as mysterious, as she is capable of handling multiple challenges at the same time.
She wins people over with her unorthodox way of interacting with others with soul and passion.
She is unapologetic about her high sense of confidence, intellectual and emotional maturity.
She attracts individuals across race, culture, sexuality, nationality, gender and social class.
She has been denied opportunities despite her intellectual giftedness, because she is a woman.
She is tender, sweet and tough at the same time. Men from all races and ethnicities eroticize her.

She moves in spiral when involved in romantic encounter as well as in intellectual debates.

She keeps it real; she can be blunt at times, and very sensitive to people's feelings other times. She is different. As a result, she has been called the dark horse who does business late at night.

Worse yet, she has been accused of sleeping with multiple partners, including with married men.

But she has freed herself from stigma; she is called all kind of names but she still holds on.

She can be a rebel today and a sheep the next day, as she changes throughout time and space.

She faces courageously the violence of time normalized and regulated by the patriarchal system.

She runs extremely low in resentment but high in human compassion and love for humanity.

At times, she acts like a tiger ready to fight sexist and capitalists trying to eat her soul.

She has a strong sense of self-pride mistaken for overconfidence and even self-importance.

Spiritual forces have helped her cope with deep psychological injury caused by male patriarchy.

She is thankful to the universe for giving her strength to fight against poverty and classism.

She pays no mind to unfounded criticism, as she keeps moving forward with self-assurance.

She is mother earth, for all lives are from her. She nourishes children of all colors and genders.

Yet these children have sometimes done her wrong in ways that often go unnoticed to the public.

She has given much more to humanity than she has received; she is giving, loving, and caring.

And yet she has been often misunderstood, undermined, underestimated, and even mistreated.

But she is too full of life to allow race, gender, and class-based oppression kill her spirit.

She always bounces back inch by inch each time she falls short in the male court of life.

She believes, deeply loves, caringly nurtures, dreams, suffers with courage and resilience.

And she fights with spiritual strength and passionately inspires people beyond borders.
She is a mother, wife, daughter, sister, lawyer, niece, senator, secretary of state, learner, artist, student, state representative, dancer, writer, athlete, entrepreneur, nurse, journalist, nurse aid, housekeeper, administrator, poet and a teacher who never stops reinventing herself.
She is a mother who lovingly gives and genuinely cares for all children.
A strong woman who chooses hope over despair, who survives miscarriages and cancer.
A woman who loves music and likes to shake her buddy; a woman with a big smile and soul.
She is a mother who still mourns the murder of her black sons and daughters by police officers.
She challenges the legal system while praying for her children to come back home from prison.
She is the spouse who still cares for her partner or husband even when she is pissed,
And a daughter who cares for her mother and father taken away from her because of addiction.
A sister who always looks out for her relatives, neighbors, and strangers;
A committed teacher who gives undivided time and attention to her students.
She is a niece, an aunt, a sister, and a cousin that friends and family members can count on.
She is a woman who floats no matter where she happens to be and what she is doing.

CHAPTER 16

Still Standing in Front of You

Here we are, standing in front of you, in your face, quite visible.
Yet, because of your racial prejudice, we have been made invisible.
Yes, we're differently embodied in a black or brown skin
Which, according to you, is too dark, unfit, and unclean.

We're standing in front you smiling, in good mood, and happy.
You only see us through our hair, which you labeled as too nappy.
And, worse, you have called our people "ancestors of savage race,"
Whose real history has yet to be fully told and really retraced.

We're standing in front of you with a different cultural background.
You only see us through our face, which you say is too flat and round.
You even say that our face must originate from the African continent,
Which you have historically misrepresented and treated with discontent.

We're standing in front of you with a different historical and cultural trajectory.
You only see us through your gross ignorance about our religion and history,
Which you have called barbarous claiming it does not deserve your time and attention.
You refuse to admit that you have silenced our history with your ideology and action.

We're standing in front of you speaking in our tongue you labeled as subaltern language.
You only see us through our accent, which you have called heavy like luggage.
We, on the other hand, respect your accent, which has awakened our curiosity.
But you say that we will never be able to speak like those from your rich city.

We're standing in front of you with multiple identities socially constructed.
You only see us through your assumptions and in ways that are fully distorted.
You tell your friend that you're disgusted with our strange physical appearance.
Your words and actions have caused us many wounds and the deepest nuisance.

We're standing in front of you with a different look, including our height.
You say our height and our dark skin prevent you from seeing us at night.
You go on to talk about our weight, which you find heavy, yet sexually appealing.
And, when it is convenient, you come around and tell us that we're your darling.

We're standing in front of you with a different set of ideology and worldview.
You only see us through yours and refuse to consider any other point of view.
You have used all strategies to portray us as barbarous, savage, and brutal.
But your misrepresentation of our people is fruitless and even hysterical.

We're standing in front of you, you look at us and dare ask us if we're illegal.
You call us dirty immigrants because we ask you if your grandparents were legal.
You only see us through distorted images about people from our native country.
You place us in a box in which our people have been sealed for more than a century.

Human up! That way, you can see us beyond our differences seen as otherness.
Human up will cause neither you nor us any pain or distress.
Instead, it will help us to be humanly close to one other.
That way, you will not look at us and treat us as the *other*.

CHAPTER 17

In Memory of George Floyd

A branch of an African tree hit intentionally by a cruel racist machine and died.
Racist laws have allowed this machine to run through red lights about which it lied.
This machine recently run over *George Floyd* over an insignificant legal matter.
With impunity, as if Black Lives, like other lives, in its evil eyes, do not matter.

George's murder has already been the seed of a global racial revolution.
The oppressed stand up across the United States, Europe, Africa, and Across the nation.
This is a revolution by the people and for the people who believe in social justice for all.
Blacks, Whites, and Browns are included, and they are fighting for the liberation of all.

The revolution has been televised, and we do not need the corporate media's presence.
When people take to the street to demand justice, the mainstream media is retrieved to silence.
George's spirit has been the guiding light in the fight against white supremacy,
While his soul is the oxygen, which has empowered us to fight it with no mercy.

His blood triggers white rage and fear as people of color everywhere protesting.
And his innocence gives us the courage to face pepper sprays thrown at us for nothing.
We have been kicked day and night by police officers but we will not be demoralized.
We have been jailed and have paid unfair files but we are not psychologically paralyzed.

We will get there. We will be free, free at last in this so-called democratic republic.

Free from a police state that treats us as if we're enemy number ONE in the eyes of the public.

We will not concede to injustice until we find justice in this land where racism is alive.

We will continue to hope and fight for a better future because we refuse to just survive.

CHAPTER 18

How It Feels to Be Black in the Americas

We're the descendants of African slaves thrown and sunk in the ocean of Whiteness.
Since the slave trade landing us to the Americas, we had been left in an inhumane mess.
During slavery our ancestors labored on their indigenous lands colonized by the Whites.
The slave masters and their descendants are all profiteers of the denial of the slaves' rights.

We are seen as a threat to Whites because we're part multiracial growing groups.
They send racist soldiers everywhere, on the street, in public parks, in troops,
To brutalize us with dogs, horses, and with all sorts of awful legalized weapons.
Yet, they say, we're the ones terrorizing people on the streets as thugs and pawns.

We're being murdered by police officers everywhere, as if it was our last day on our land,
Where licensed murderers supported by the government and red necks from the mainland,
Who believe in their guns, have provoked and murdered innocent Blacks and Browns,
Whom they label as thugs, savages, and criminals that are invading their towns.

From the tree to the street, Blacks have been lynched by licensed murders with impunity,
While political pundits of all creeds are talking about the economy but not racial unity.
The law does not protect us; the neighbor and the person on street are calling the police on us.
We are not safe anywhere in this great nation built by slaves, our ancestors, who are all of us.

© PIERRE W. ORELUS, 2022 | DOI:10.1163/9789004525467_019

Yet we're told to go back to Africa, our mother land, which they still colonize and occupy.
It is no longer the land we were forced to leave behind; it has become a Euro/American pie,
Which they have enjoyed in a Black continent they despise but stay there because it is fertile.
European invaders colonized that land now ruled by African neo-colonizers who are as hostile.

We're killed by weapons, visible and invisible, while we're on the street protesting.
Yet they say it is Black and Brown killing each other. Isn't that argument interesting?
We remain immobile in their bestial arms strangling us, yet we're accused of resisting arrest.
"We can't breathe," we say with tears, but nobody seems to care, as we lie down on our chest.

Black lives matter like all lives, but ours have been taken away with impunity by Whites.
We're afraid of calling the police to protect us, and it does not matter if we are right.
We have no place to hide, for we're too Black or too Brown to fool their blue or brown eyes.
We must fight in order to live for ourselves and future generations of all skin colors and eyes.

CHAPTER 19

We're Rising up in Multi Colors

We are no longer silent in front of white terror and white supremacy.
We march, demonstrate, and occupy the street, and we ask for no mercy.
We're rising up in multi colors and great numbers climbing the freedom hill.
We are on their faces while they are pulling out their guns to shoot and kill.

They accuse us of destroying stores and buildings that we do not even own.
We live in their buildings and we consume things that are not our own.
We rent from them, shop in their stores, buy their food and eat in their restaurants,
While we stand up to political pundits and White civilians with their racist rants.

Some White people believe that Blacks who are revolting are trouble makers and thugs,
Who are stealing White people's properties while daring ask those who pass by for hugs.
We are not like White KKK terrorists who are on the street creating all kinds of mess.
They are lucky, for we Blacks are not seeking revenge, but rather justice and fairness.

CHAPTER 20

Love Always Trumps over Hate

Darling, do not worry, love always trumps over injustice and hate.
With your brilliant mind, amazing personality, and sweet heart,
You are the most refined human being on the planet in my soul.
Motherhood will make you even more beautiful and radiant in my eyes.
The way you take care of your-self and your loved ones are unique.
You make me want to be the best father and partner on this planet.
For your compassion and kindness, I will go straight down on your knee,
Whereas for your moves and beautiful smile, I will walk a billion miles.
To your sense of forgiveness and support, I am forever very grateful.
Darling, the future looks bright, despite some clouds in our native land.
Love always trumps over aversion and bitterness, and I deeply feel it inside.
Do not look behind, regardless of the greatest forms of violence of our time.
With love, we're already on your way to collective victory over hatred.

CHAPTER 21

I Am Black, and I Am Enough!

I listen carefully to my deep emotions for self-control and inner peace.
I feel safe, healthy, grateful, and happy, as I am living life in its full moon.
I love myself and other human beings, and I am loving in my own way.
I am a caring parent, brother, uncle, friend, cousin, sister, aunt, mother, and neighbor.
I am amazingly positive, peaceful, fun, kind, sensitive, and empathetic.
I respect and value other human beings as I respect and value myself.
I am a smart, kind, loving, generous, loyal, and resilient person who cherishes family.
I am generous, wealthy, forgiving, compassionate, and successful in my own way.
I am thankful for the persons I love and choose to be with for the rest of my life.
I am co-raising healthy, smart, kind, confident, strong, and successful children of all colors.
I am a gifted, creative, interesting, easy and a complex person at the same time.
I am motivated, authentic, persistent, forgiving, enthusiastic, and a visionary.
I am confident, charming, handsome, strong, friendly, generous, and sociable.
I am a successful writer, doctor, nurse, scholar, teacher, athlete, politician, scientist,
artist, entrepreneur, business person, engineer, singer, dancer, actor, and philanthropist.
I am from a family root that gives birth to African families who have shaped world history.
I am Black, and I am enough!

CHAPTER 22

How Real Love Feels Like

For those who have been deeply disappointed and hurt,
Love can feel like a dirty word, even a bloody one.
A word that can makes one vulnerable in the mouth of a beast,
Which changes color constantly to meet its self-serving needs,
Which must be met at any cost, even if this necessitates sabotaging the
Reputation of its partner, for an animal is only loyal to its needs.

Love is real when it is both felt and demonstrated through genuine action.
It is not based on conditions serving the interests of a self-righteous party,
Who, through ingenuine smiles, fools others serving their own interests.
Real love does not label or control in order to satisfy one's selfish needs.

When the word love is used to execute one's personal hidden material agenda,
It can be deeply experienced and felt like a dirty and even a bloody word.
Gold diggers use the word love only for their selfish advancements,
At the expense of those who are honest, and genuinely trust them.

Do not seek or cry for love as it is not and can't be found outside.
Real love is nowhere to be found but within, in us, in our inner-self.
One's inner self can, and does intuitively and genuinely look for real love,
Which can also be found in all people, regardless of their gender, sex, and social class.
But appreciation, however deep, is not love, because it fades away overtime.

Real love does not die, for it always bounces back like a reed, regardless of the weather.
But conditional, self-serving and made-believe types of love evaporates in tough times.

True love is like a bird who flies through the four seasons and comes out refreshed to begin Again; it does not manipulate, assault or denigrate the other for the sake of saving one's face.

Real love genuinely forgives, as we all live with our human imperfection. It does not betray, nor does it suck one's bone and trash it when it is no longer needed.
Pathological abusive behavior and action masked through deceiving smiles is not love.
Real love liberates, embraces truth, rejects pretenses, and is shown through genuine action.

CHAPTER 23

The COVID-19 Pandemic of Color

The COVID-19 pandemic hits the heart of the world with a bloody hand. Hospitals are crowded and overloaded with very sick individuals as well as dead people, particularly people of color, piled up in black bags, normally used for trash, ready to be thrown away.

Family members are crying hard as they do not get to say goodbye to their loved ones,
While workers who lost their jobs are waiting in long lane to apply for unemployment,
Which is already insufficient to respond to the needs of the poor and the middle.

Most places, particularly schools, churches, gyms, night clubs, bars, and restaurants, are closed.
People are forcibly stuck in their houses with family members, including infected ones. With a deep sense of hope mixed with broken hearts and lively souls, people exclaim: we need help!

Many of whom eventually die hopelessly, while politicians, who are running their race for power,
Promise all kinds of solutions but none seems promising to slow or end the pandemic,
Which has killed disproportionally poor people of color, among the most vulnerable group.

We need love, respect, equity, equality, and peace for all!
Many have been searching day and night for a magic love,
Which they have in them but doubt it because of believed fear.

The pandemics are ravaging families around the world of various backgrounds.
Some families have kept love alive, while others have broken up.
Still others have found their new soulmates during this crisis.

CHAPTER 24

Love Is All That We Need

Love is all that we need,
So goes the old saying.
We have been listening to our inner voice
To feel and understand the meaning embedded in this adage.
Alone, awaiting to find one's missing half,
Who has, too, long waited with a deep sense of hope,
One asks: can true love be found along with respect,
Trust, honesty, fidelity, understanding, and compassion?

Love alongside honesty and transparency are not appreciated sometime.
They are taken for granted by ungrateful individuals of all colors,
And sexes and genders, who often lack conscience and fairness,
And integrity and sincerity that they often claim they have,
Although, like other human beings, they, too, possess some good qualities.

Some people suffer in silence to maintain their integrity and protect partners' privacy.
Hence, experiencing a lack of trust in a toxic relationship feels like drinking a silent poison.
Suddenly life is back again, vividly renewed with solar energy and unconditional love,
And with a fresh air going through our human flesh,
Which is not tainted by toxicity, like envy and jealousy,
And human hypocrisy hidden through phony smiles.

Hope is born again to help you meet your soul mate unexpectedly
To live a life together without fights, betrayals, and self-serving plans,
With the interference of family members and friends in a closeted manner.
No more self-righteous, self-serving, and psychopathic tendencies
And deceitful actions from those who pretend to be angel, innocent.

Genuine love is found in the other self in flesh,
I mean an amazing, loving, kind, flexible, generous,

Honest, and intellectually sophisticated person,
With whom one feels like living in a *magic land*,
Which is bright, unique and transformative.

No need to be angry or sad and keep your guard on,
At all time, for love is here, not on the way.
Relax. Your other half got your back for real,
And it is not for self-serving needs and interests.

Life is back with love in its full moon and sunshine,
After years of cold winters feeling lonely in a relationship
And raising children while at the same time trying to maintain a career.
Be ready to begin to love again, with a whole heart and soul,
With a wonderful person, whose inner qualities are rare to combine.

You will not need the state regulated marriage rules;
They won't work for you, for you are free individuals,
Who want to live your love in a non-conformist fashion.
As you face life vicissitudes, think about courage, respect,
Trust, faithfulness, forgiveness and, above all, love.

CHAPTER 25

Raising Queer Teens

Parenting is a good and beautiful challenge,
Which comes in waves and never ends.
It is both predictable and unpredictable.

It makes one happy all the time in one's heart,
And frustrated at times when dealing with disciplinary issues,
But parenting is not and can't be tradable, for it is priceless.

It is like feeling one's beautiful shadow wherever one is;
Parenting is inescapable and eternal;
Hence, it can't be avoided.

Indeed, parenting feels like seeing one's self shown through another veil,
Which looks and feels real, day and night, inside and out,
Even when it might not be visible to people and society.

Parenting a child of a different sexual orientation is challenging.
Indeed, it is a terrific and ongoing challenge,
Especially when it started at an early stage, say preteen.
It is many parents' reality, both straight and non-straight.
It can be more challenging, particularly for parents of a different sexual orientation.
That is, for parents who only know how to feel and be straight, inside and out.
Indeed, it is challenging raising children who are sexually different.
Yet with this new challenge comes lots of beauty, both visible and unknown.

Communication is sometimes blocked due to gender and sexual differences,
Yet they need to be negotiated and accepted as a reality by both straight parents and queer teens.

Some parents do not feel that they have awareness to understand their children' sexual orientation, while other family members, perhaps out of concern and care, exacerbate the situation with their unexamined homophobia.

Hope, prayers, and affirmation along with spiritual meditation can be helpful,
But they do not stop the mental breakdown, shown and hidden, that queer teens, including preteens, often experience.

Parenting in itself is challenging, and people's prejudice makes more challenging raising queer teens, for situations encountered at home often reflect the outside world reality,
which teens daily face and parents often ignore.

Homophobia and transphobia prevent queer people from living
life in its full moon and plain day light.
These systemic forms of oppression must go,
And parents raising queer teens deserve world respect.

CHAPTER 26

Cancer Sucks!

"I did not get to send her flowers as I planned,"
I sadly said to myself when I learned that she transitioned.
I kept saying to myself, I'll have time, as I have been
busy taking care of my children and wrapped up by work.
She is a fighter, I said. She will not go anytime soon.
I had even hoped to see her at the AERA conference next year.
But I was done wrong by the false hope of time
Whose violence has caused me such an illusion.
She is gone. Too soon. Cancer sucks! I said out loud.
She was a dear colleague who showed nothing but sincerity and kindness,
and willingness to support others as she was battling cancer.
Ashe Rochelle Brock! You're dearly missed,
We'll meet again when our time to transition comes.

CHAPTER 27

The Death of the Nation

This great nation is slowly dying,
Due to seemingly unresolved inner discord and human greed.
Class, race, religion, and sexual division, and oppression of all kinds incessantly occur,
While politicians are attacking one another to gain political momentum to get [r]elected.

Racists believe they are right in their criminal mind to kill,
And so, they harm civilians of color opposing their terrorist acts.
Meanwhile, neo-liberal and conservative groups criticize progressive people who
Take to the street to counter violent action of Alright, White Supremacist groups.

Yet conservatives and defenders of neoliberalist and racist systems criticize them,
Claiming tearing everything apart does not serve the American neoliberal economy,
As if such rhetoric reflects the reality of historically marginalized groups,
Namely poor Blacks, poor Whites, and other poor people of color who are left behind.

Main point missing from debates is often the obvious one.
That is, the nation is dying due to greed,
Often race-, class-, gender-, and sex-based.
The motor that keeps running the racist, capitalist, and sexist machine is greed.

The source of the destruction of the health system and the environment is greed,
And the main source of corruption of our rigged political system is greed.
Conflicts between citizens of all colors are partially fueled by greed.
In brief, the cause of the early death of the nation is greed.

© PIERRE W. ORELUS, 2022 | DOI:10.1163/9789004525467_028

CHAPTER 28

When Love Is Gone

When one's heart hurts, so does the rest of one's entire self.
When there is neither respect nor trust in a relationship, love is no more.
All of sudden, sadness, regrets, remorse, and pain start emerging,
From the subconscious to the conscious.

All seems dark even in the midst of light, however bright or dim.
It is all blurry; the past becomes a daily shadow that follows you,
Wherever you go and whoever you are, and whatever you're doing.
It does not matter if you're sitting, walking, running, reading, writing, or eating.

It feels like nothing else can be done, for all is already broken.
The known is painful, so is the unknown, as there is no clear road ahead.
Your brain spins like a wheel turned incessantly,
For it is not rested enough to think with clarity.

Broken relationships feel like a game that has been lost.
But one still hopes to win it at any cost.
Emotions start flowing like a waterfall on one's human psychological reservoir,
Which is made of love and compassion but also filled with guilt, disappointments,
resentment, anger, and even rage.

When relationships are broken and love is gone,
It feels as if one is living in constant winter
With little hope for a return to spring and summer.
All seems dark and chaotic but it is only temporary,
For true love is already on the way waiting for the right energy
to connect at its own time and space.

CHAPTER 29

The Fear of Death

Many underlying factors, known and unknown,
Cause the deep fear of death in some people,
Both young and old.
People are afraid of dying generally,
Including the poor, the rich,
The straight and the gay;
The White and the Black;
The abled and the disabled;
The loyal and the traitor;
The realist and the dreamer;
The pessimist and the optimist;
The tall and the short;
The famous and the unknown;
Children and adults;
Men, women, and trans-people;
And those who do not fit in these labels.
Few of us might not be afraid of dying,
But most of us are frightened by the mere idea of it.
The fear of not fulfilling one's own mission on this earth
Before the inevitable final transition is death in itself.
Death itself should not be fearful, as it is awaiting all of us.
Like all living creatures, we will all transition one day.
Before we do, let's aim to give it all for humanity,
On this physical earth, while our spirit will continue to live
For the protection of our loved ones and others in need.

CHAPTER 30

How to Spot a Psychopath

Psychopaths usually craft self-serving, twisted narratives to save face,
As if parents, relatives, and friends expect them to protect it face by any cost,
including sabotaging the name and reputation of honest people that seem vulnerable.
Their smiles are not to be trusted because they are nothing but performance for survival.

Insults and lies are coded in carefully crafted languages to wound the spirit of people
Whose names they conveniently use for self-serving purposes and those of their families.
Psychopaths come in all genders, races, sexes religion, and social classes.
They tend to be very warm with a seemingly genuine smile intentionally aimed to fool.
Appearance, comfort, and selfish interests are their key priorities.

Psychopaths are not afraid of tainting people's reputation merely to save their face.
People other than other their family members and close friends do not matter,
Except in empty speeches on social justice, equity, diversity and equality.
Their co-dependent relatives tend to be their confidents and their rocks.
For they have been part of the same toxic web since childhood.

They plot things in secret while showing in public a fake smile to fool others.
Psychopaths are vampires; they suck people's blood for their uncontrolled needs.
They destroy for self-righteous and self-serving needs and wants,
And for false sense of financial safety for themselves and their co-conspirators.

They have neither soul nor compassion for others, especially those who dare challenge them.

They are human beings in form and shape but monsters in spirit and soul,
Which they often reveal through their evil actions, both subtle and overt.
Psychopaths are created by society, although some claim they are born as such.
Regardless, they are to be avoided by all costs, for they merely use people to get ahead.

CHAPTER 31

You're a Beautiful Wave

You're a beautiful wave that keeps coming,
That can't be unseen because you're irresistibly beautiful.
You're the wave that comes with different vibes,
Each time with a renewed hope,
Waiting for time to discern its genuine effects on your soul,
With kindness, compassion, and love shown for the people,
Particularly the traumatized and the oppressed.

You're a beautiful wave that comes with its complexity each season:
Winter, spring, summer, and fall.
And the cycle continues, with its seasonal temperature presented as challenges.
Yet you have never been dried of love, kindness, and compassion for others.

You're a beautiful wave that comes with a renewed spirit,
In search of the salvation of a hurtful and haunting past,
From which stems a deep sense of hope for the present and the future,
Yet often disturbed by recurrences of old memories triggered and demonstrated in flesh,
Through displayed anger and resentment meshed in self-pride and sense of human dignity.
These emotions give the ego the illusion that it is safe from human experiences subject to conflicts As well as resentment and anger held against perceived enemies seen as others.

You're a beautiful wave on a spiritual journey for the recovery of your own self wounded,
And temporarily lost in pleasing, loving, and balancing the lives of other family members,
Who are lost themselves in their own search of salvation, as they are aging and declining,
And who are seemingly full of regrets and deep-seated resentments against others, whom,

They believe to be the source of their emotional challenges and physical illnesses.

You're a beautiful wave that brings sunshine to the sea and ocean of people needy for love
And attention, which you, too, need and crave for, like all human beings.
Yet you keep giving love unconditionally at the expense of your own reservoir,
Which contains not only the warm water you throw kindly at people's face,
But also your radiant smile, which brings light to the human soul.

While you're searching your own path and salvation from a hurtful past.
Your human wave keeps coming, and shines people's souls and spirit.
You're not only a wave but also the fountain from which stems the spring water your loved ones, among others, drink daily, and from which you're inspiring hope for many, known and unknown.

CHAPTER 32

On Co-Parenting

Love, time, money, and energy invested in co-parenting are worth the price,
Even though attention given to details can be overwhelming at times, but still worth it.
When love is gone between parents, children become or should become the supreme priority.
Parental love is unconditional, whereas marriage is nothing but a legalized social contract.

Children from separated or divorced parents matter beyond the end term of their parents' marriage, So, they must be well taken care of regardless of their parents' ego war.
Many divorced couples have been involved in all kinds of conflicts that are ego driven.
Yet some blame their partners for cheating, even though they are cheaters themselves.

They cheat on their partner, in closet, even with people of opposite sex,
While claiming a heterosexual identity to pimp the queer movement.
Parenting is not ideal but can be worked out with respectful, honest, and fair parents.
Manipulative, dishonest, unfair, and self-serving parents can make it a harsher task.

No children should be caught in their parents' business.
But it is becoming a reality as a result of separation and divorce.
For many parents, co-parenting sucks,
While for others, it is a reality they accept.

Either way, it is the children who ultimately pay the heaviest price of poor co-parenting.
No one was married to be separated or divorced, but the violence of time has caused it.
After all, co-parenting is temporary, for children grow up to become adults.
Parents are adults, so they will eventually move on and live their lives.

CHAPTER 33

The Depressed

Some have seen, known, and experienced depression,
In all its colors and dimension, hidden and exposed, real and imagined.
Some have survived it, while others have succumbed to it.
Still others are simply physically present on this earth.

Depression can be gene-related, and also stems from cruelty experienced overtime.
Specifically, it can be the end result of systemic oppression endured leading to mental illnesses.
Regardless of its root, depression has caused mental damages to people and society.
Depressed people can be really harmful to themselves, loved ones, and others.

Depression is degenerative and causes a lack of interest in life events outside the depressive world.
It leads to isolation, mental self-destruction, and suicide thoughts when the sense of hope is gone.
But it is often hidden through shinny smiles and false sense of happiness
Projected on the outside world for the acceptance of others.

Indeed, some forms of depression are hidden through false images projected on the outside world.
And yes, depressed people tend to present a false sense of themselves to the judgmental world,
As they struggle to accept their past and present reality faced in their inner life and outer world.
They often present their misery who take over themselves in codes, which can be hard to decode.

Systemic forms of oppression and depression are intimately interwoven.
Yet this fact has been overlooked by psychologists and therapists, except a few.

The world itself has been a depressive place, and has consequently affected people,
Regardless of their race, ethnicity, gender, class, sex, age, sexuality, and religion.

CHAPTER 34

Discovering African Spirituality

I believed in the White Jesus because my mother told me to do so.
After I left home for school outside the country side,
I lost such faith as I discovered my African root.

I rejected the White Jesus I used to believe in.
I transitioned from White Christianity to African spirituality.
I now believe in African spirit and Voodoo.

The discovery of my spiritual root has been immensely beneficial.
Such discovery has helped me believe in myself spiritually more than ever before.
My ancestors' spirit continues living and being manifested through the body of their children.

CHAPTER 35

On Forgiveness

Forgive more and more to liberate oneself, says the wise woman.
Forgiving is necessary to end self-infringing mental misery from resentment and anger.
Smart people forgive because they want to live peacefully, happy, and long.
Those who are unforgiving tend to be vindictive, miserable and toxic.

Forgiveness is a gift often hard to give to one self and others.
Yet it is necessary to do so for human growth and the survival of the global community.
Forgive as one wishes to be forgiven to lighten one's heart,
And for the restoration of inner and collective peace.

CHAPTER 36

Living in the Future

When the present is not deeply felt,
And the past start to feel like a shadow,
One is inspired to live in the future,
So as to keep nourishing hopes and staying alive.

Living in the future is not an escape from the present reality,
But a continuous mental journey to continuously know one's self,
Hurt by inequities in society, as well as betrays and lies experienced,
With politicians and so-called loved ones, including family and friends.

Life in the present can feel at times like a battlefield, yet we have to continue to live.
Living in the future then becomes a survival skill learned through life struggles.
And it can help imagine a better life for one's self and a better world for humanity.
Isn't what we all need to feel that we're living on this earth, not existing?

CHAPTER 37

In Honor of Our Black Ancestors

The Day of the dead is approaching; it is around the corner.
People are preparing their rituals to celebrate their loved ones,
Who have transitioned from the visible to the invisible world.

Supposedly, our ancestors can't be seen physically.
But they are here, and we feel them in our soul.
They are felt and can be seen upon special invocation.

My grand-parents and great grand-parents, among others,
Are here, with me; yet they all have been transitioned for decades.
I feel them, and they feel me; isn't a unique feeling?

I feel protected, and surveilled at the same time, for I can't misbehave.
But where are they? They are here, there, everywhere, in spirit.
No need to see them to believe it, for because one feels, therefore one believes.

I feel my ancestors as they are all invisibly present in front of me.
It is worth honoring them, for they're our eternal protection
From unknown and known negative forces in this imperfect world.

CHAPTER 38

The Beauty in Solitude

Solitude can be a gift or a curse depending on how it comes and how it's dealt with.
Solitude at times rejuvenates one's soul, at times withers it, and at times kills it.
And yet solitude gives one a unique chance, a unique place to be still, and to grow.
A chance to be the authentic person one ever wanted to be or deserves to be.

Solitude brings with it an ocean of profound emotions, at times overpowering.
Solitude can bring happiness and joy; it can also bring sadness and melancholy.
But such feelings are always on the move; they come and go; and they float.
They float in one's mind like the waves in the ocean and the clouds in the sky.

Solitude creates an oxygenic zone for self-contemplation, meditation, and self-reflection.
Solitude also creates space for self-examination and a self-to-self-confrontation.
Solitude brings at times lightness and at times darkness, both during day and at night.
Solitude teaches us how to appreciate even more human presence and human touch in the flesh.

Solitude forcibly puts us in a situation to face our fear of being alone.
Solitude compels people to examine both their inner and outer selves.
Indeed, solitude challenges one to be in deep touch with oneself.
Solitude also forces us to think about and, at times, reflect on the "other."

Solitude leads to healthy or troubled thoughts, like self-affirmation and/or self-destruction.

Solitude gives us the space to reflect on and confront one's mistakes, downfalls, and successes.

Indeed, solitude allows one to retrace one's life trajectory, including one's life joyful events.

Solitude gives one the space to reflect on and pick one's broken pieces and rebuild one's life.

PART 2

Black Beauty, Love, and Healing

CHAPTER 39

Where Is the God for Black People?

Mother earth, nothing less than an individual
Thinking that this duty is due to him
To speak to you. Here I am.
All alone I'm here
Inside a tiny room of a house
Inspiring me, however, the reason
To invoke your name, not to challenge you,
And to know if you have fun dozing off,
Since a lot of black people
Are still honking their horns
With the hope that you hear them,
Because they do not want to waste time
In a foolish belief
Which now makes them weary.
I do not want to lose faith,
Please tell me the real laws,
Laws of liberty, justice, wisdom, and light
After which, I will say good prayers.
Not wanting to name you sir,
And to be sure that you're in heaven,
Tell me, if you are listening and are willing to help me
Accomplish my mission on this earth.
I walk on a lot of religions
Professing their faith to different regions.
Not knowing what they are doing,
I cannot discover their depths.
God: the father, the son and the holy spirit.
As for me, I'm completely puzzled
By these words that seem incomprehensible to me
And that no one can make justifiable.
Beloved, wherever you are,
Dressed in a coat or a silk dress,
Either white, red, yellow or black
Enthroning in a castle or in a corridor,
I beg you to explain these words to me

That cause me so much pain.
They have certainly been explained in the Bible.
But they seem incomprehensible to me.
Are you really our guide?
So why is everything so rigid to us?
If you exist, give us the secret of life
Which we really want.
Are you the wind, the dust or the air?
Why not a glimmer of your light?
So should I believe in the wind
That bothers me very often?
Should I believe in a supreme being
Not knowing if he's even looking at me?
Should I throw myself into the adventure
While ignoring the laws of nature?
Mother earth, in short God,
Since we call you God.
If frankly you want us on your land,
Grant us this great wish:
Project us, we the Blacks, your light.

CHAPTER 40

Black Exodus

Why black hunger, in short, misery
Forcing us to go to the sea
Without food, without any destination,
And yet, we are a nation?

Why all these words: unemployment and poverty,
Which very often make us angry?
Why caste, tribal conflicts, and gender inequality,
Corollaries of poverty and ferocity, which force us to flee our countries?

Why can't we smile and dance with life?
Why suffer and even die in the sea?
Die, by whom? By God or by nature?
Or by the ferocity of a dictatorship and monarchy?

Why the wickedness, the killing
That is done under a pillory in our native land?
Why aristocracy and autocracy?
Why not make democracy grow?

Why the gospel of resignation from the Christian preacher
Aimed to make us become submissive?
Why is the universe turning its face on us?
Don't we also have a fair place on this earth?

If the messiah created us with purity and taste,
So why do they want to throw us into the sewer both at home and overseas?
Finally, why individualism and egoism?
Why not humanitarianism?

Why black exodus from violence of poverty and human greed
If exist sharing and fraternity?
Sharing and fraternity being just words
That smear people with false reasoning.

Why black exodus, poverty and misery,
Which put Blacks in both the Third and the First world
Under this hypocritical and grinning blue sky?
Doesn't it all seem filthy, corrupt and threatening?

Why are too many Blacks born in the stench of poverty,
And then grow up and go through begging?
Is it the wish of nature or of the sky?
Or the iniquitous sharing of honey of the earth?

Black Exodus, is it not the result,
Wherever, in any part of Africa, Europe or the Americas,
Of the enjoyment of a well-breastfed child
To the prejudice of his abused mother?

Oh! without a doubt. The Black third eyes see
Masked birds of prey using all kinds of voices
Winning the honesty and the soul of the people
In order to suck the essence of their blood.

CHAPTER 41

Open Letter to Our Ancestors

Very dear those who passed away,
You who had, of course, passed,
courageously, from the physical life to the spiritual one
Trying to break down a lot of ramparts.
Now on this physical earth
There is only injustice and misery for us.
Perhaps, during your time, long ago,
You tasted the honey of paradise there.
As for us, heirs of this land,
In which we have found ourselves
To be part of in this new era,
We have only known under this grimacing sky
Nothing but nausea, repugnance and gall.
Earthly food being indivisible,
For us: it's the crumb. O charitable ancestors!
So what do we need to do
So that can stop?
We are told every day to wait and pray.
Bitterly, we even try to scream.
Unfortunately, our cries do not reach the top
Where is, perhaps, God or Muhammad.
So, dear ancestors, what is the right way
To take, if we want our voice
To be heard everywhere
So that we could claim what belongs to us?
We are between the anvil and the hammer.
So, we necessarily need your coat
To protect us from the wind of human selfishness
Preventing us from practicing altruism.

CHAPTER 42

Only the Truth Will Set us Free

On the way to the truth,
Always strewn with obstacles and obscurity.
Is there at least a ray of both hope and light
That may constitute our perfect mirror?

The truth that comes from the bottom of the soul
Wounds, of course. But it is an excellent weapon.
The truth should be a compass of everything,
Even when we can possibly suffer from it.

How infamous is it to feed on lies,
That depersonalizes, obscures, falsifies and eats us away?
The truth, purity of conscience,
Should be the epitome
Of every man or woman, or of every individual
Because it is humanly due to us.

Why be afraid to openly tell the truth
When it comes to transforming humanity?
For where the truth is advocated, the light is shed,
Anywhere, in any region or country.

The truth is the dawn of spring.
She is young at all times.
Being the ideal reference for transformative change,
She judges everyone fairly.

The free person is truthful.
However, he, she or they must also be scientific
Because, to indulge, to orient oneself towards science,
Means to free one's mind and conscience.

For journalists, teachers, and credible lawyers,
The truth can make their task easy, possible,

Without ignoring the fact that they can suffer from it,
And they can even become martyrs.

The truth is sometimes bitter and honeyed.
Honeyed, because it makes life bright.
Bitter, because it unmasks the hypocrisy
And, subsequently, causes hatred and heresy.

To avoid a life full of lies and darkness,
We must tell the truth, especially if we want to spread light.
Whether it is at the cost of one's life or one's existence,
Which is prone to human suffering.

CHAPTER 43

Involuntary Exile

O infamous involuntary exile
Often occurs on one's own land!
Excluded from all social settings,
As if we were not native.

Exiled like the needy and poor immigrants
Leaving often their countries against their will
To slave away in a foreign land!
Isn't the consequence of abject poverty!

How much life is there for these proscribed human beings
Slaving away at any time abroad in order
To help support their native relatives back home?
This experience often causes nostalgia, and that's fatal!

Often it is the coincidence of a sea voyage,
Dependent on the whim of an ocean of crime,
Crime coming from animalized boats
Aimed at causing those on board paralyzed.

They leave, these Black exiles, without having any return plane ticket
To stop being treated like the condemned of the land or vultures,
In their own land, where they were born and have relatives and many friends,
But they had to leave it because life had become an enemy to them.

Misery and poverty, you are a sacrilege, infamous!
You killed a lot of us including children and women
Selling their strength as product abroad
To exploiters without guts. Their childhood is nothing but straw.

Involuntary exiles, their lives are mutilated.
Puzzled, embittered, they dare not even speak,
Because their hearts swell with longing and hate
Resulting from frustration, humiliation and pain.

Hunted by the misery of their own country,
And in search of a place where the vital water has gushed out,
Day for them is night and night is day.
They are even deprived of the time to say hello.

It seems that nature does not belong to them,
Because sometimes they are even Christians
Who pray and others enjoy their prayers
Naively believing that the rich are for hell.

Oh all forces of nature, king of the universe!
These words that are constructed, erected in verse
Are intended to encourage them, to comfort them,
These involuntary exiles, these mistreated.

If we prone that life is union, sharing.
So why, yes why such wild life,
Led by sons and daughters, in brief children of the earth
In foreign countries where they are treated as second citizens of the earth?

CHAPTER 44

The Day of Revolt

Day of blood, of revival.
Everywhere, the people are demanding,
With all their mind and soul,
The end of all shenanigans.

Everywhere, it was a "boukman" day, THE day.
The lions behaved like a gentleman
To escape the steamroller
Designed precisely for the oppressors.

The 7th of February, in 1986, the sun had smiled
To all Haitians, once, depriving of corn, of rice
On this earth, according to the old saying,
Where there was no fair sharing.

All those overwhelming with grief
Suddenly took breath,
Thanks to this gentle and oasis of wind.
Wind of freedom which never blew before during the Duvaliers.

But unfortunately! February 7, 1986. Yes February 7, 1986!
Has turned his face on the workers,
Constituting the pillar of Haiti Thomas
Who is now in deep coma.

CHAPTER 45

Bloody Day

On that date, *29 November 1987*,
Everyone was happy
And even believed that it was time
To go throw a ballot
Around eight, nine in the morning
In search of a truth
For the well-being of a society.

Yes, it was at the street "Vaillant,"
Where brave and valiant men,
Imbued with courage and patriotism,
Were going to prove their heroism and free their minds and souls
But they were murdered by bloodthirsty people with guns.

CHAPTER 46

God, Where Are You?

Why continue to live if life is so sorrowful?
Without love, isolated like little grains
Located in the middle of a forest,
Where no one spoke.

Why existing
If everything is suffering?
If we are denied basic necessities, like food and shelter,
On what then would our survival be based?

In reflecting, one sees that in this new era
Money seems to be the only master.
Not wanting to compromise,
What should we do? Throw ourselves into the sea?

God, where are you?
We are being screwed up.
Please show us your omnipotence
That we impatiently need.

There is no life without ever knowing a day of honey,
But, instead, disappointment, gall, and suffering.
This life, we do not deserve it.
God, where are you? We desperately need you.

CHAPTER 47

The Black Child

You who represent the future for the Black world,
Why do people nearly everywhere want to betray you?
Your gaze reminds us of misery. Why?
Did you not also come from a mother?
Do they want you to languish in misery?
No, that would never be your wish.

From now on! life, this word must be taboo,
If to live, you have to wallow in the mud.
Why this proverb: everyone has a star.
Why are you homeless?
How is yours excluded from the sky?
For you, everything is finished and contrasted?

Fruit of this world! Is it your skin that betrays you?
Why this constraint: make the hedge
In a street where jumble is the only master,
And which inevitably risks compromising everything.
What will be the day of your liberation, your freedom,
Since for you, almost every day is suffering?

Why do they want you to feed of crumbs?
Why do they consider you as mute?
Have patience child! We wait for the rumble of the storm
To finally break this pyramid of exploitation
Rooted in hypocrisy, lies and manipulation.

CHAPTER 48

Dear Black Women

Dear Black Women,
Our soul,
Without you,
No joy.

True goddess
With all caress,
Your existence
Is our quintessence.

Source of poetry,
You stimulate our frenzy
In a crazy way, without end,
With your sweet hands.

Sometimes angry, yes sometimes you're angry,
But still charming
With your heart,
Key to happiness.

Servant of youth!
Without your caresses,
Life has no meaning
No matter what.

Real reference
Of Preference
For the poets
From other planets.

O Black women!
Our soul
Without you
No joy.

Even when cunning,
We cannot dare
Live without you
Because you're our zeal.

Big or small, tall or short,
We still revere you.
Isn't that beauty in itself!
What a magic love!

Whether we are misogynist,
We are your origin.
So what can we do?
Can we undo it?

Man, Woman or They,
It is life in a soul.
Here is, the ineluctable
And the unmistakable!

The bestial men plunder her
When they get angry.
Yet her resilience and gentleness
Cure all hatred and pain.

CHAPTER 49

African Goddess

You are unique. There is none like you.
My heart, my soul and my ear,
Listening to your voice of angel and nobility,
Reach the climax of joy.

You, with your lovely, jovial smile
You make me think, of course, of the morning breeze
That inspires young writers and poets
The clearest and sharpest ideas.

I have my tenderest feelings for you.
You make me ask myself sincerely:
Are you not the quintessence
Of all my being and existence?

You, who deserve to be contemplated and adored,
Should certainly, despite the tide,
Be the enjoyer of an ocean of pure love
Filled with spring flowers and adornment.

Finally, only you can fill all my voids.
I hope that for me your heart is not rigid,
So that I can be the main actor
In the theater of your life and your heart.

Adornment of the universe!
I offer you these verses
In reward
To your importance.

CHAPTER 50

Life as a Circle

Here are the dawn and the sunrise.
Soon will be the sunset.
Over here sadness, over there melody.
Being inhumane, it's a perfect comedy.
But, conscious, it's the lively heartbeat
Resulting from anger, repugnance and resentment.

Today, it is joy and gentleness
While tomorrow can only be bad luck.
Here is the sun. It is very ardent.
Everyone is on their toes.
We walk, we eat and we are happy.
But this is only for a period of time.

Life is just a game
That can sometimes put everything at stake.
And, if we try to define it,
We can even suffer from it.
Meanwhile, the only king awaits us: death,
Which causes pain, cries and remorse.

CHAPTER 51

Black Youth

What does youth empowerment really mean to
Young Blacks who suffer from systemic racism and capitalism?
Apparently portrayed as guideless and mirrorless,
Yet it is the future and the hope
Of the world, particularly the next generation.

The Black youth is not naive.
That's why it gets impatient
For a freedom and liberty that it claims,
Wherever it might be, with all its soul,
And with a spirit of solidarity.

Liberty and freedom are synonymous with life.
On what would their survival be based if we deprived Black youth of them?
They suffer while speaking of justice and democracy,
Despite all the frustration and twists.

Is life about suffering and dying?
No. There is still an alternative way to explore, that is, the path
Where all young people of all colors work together
For the granting of human dignity, democracy, justice, liberty and freedom.

CHAPTER 52

I Have Another Dream

I have another dream to speak, to express myself in verses
To exhort the oppressed
To free themselves from the yoke of slavery
That the exploiters make use of
To stock up and get rich.

I would like to be the heart of the left behind
Who may not even be aware
Of their misery, of their inhumane life,
And who, nevertheless, rush to say "amen"
To Sunday sermons not even aimed at liberating them.

I would like to settle on the side of the sheep
To tell them to drop that old tone,
The tone of docility, of naivety
So that they stop being exploited.

I would like to be the universe messenger
Without the intention of behaving and setting myself up as a god,
And without being overwhelmed with feelings of hatred, revenge or resignation
In order to preach its word of life, including hope and liberation.

Light in Hope

I would like that hatred, famine and injustice
Give way to love, fairness, kindness, and justice
So that infantile death and wickedness
Stop happening in the world.

I would like the biggest bird, the Austria, the eagle
To stop hovering over the little ones to violate their rules
That their ancestors so worthily established
And which should never be forgotten.

I would like to caress and help concretize,
Without a second thought, without tiring,
The dreams of the workers and the farmers
Suffering for many years.

I would finally like to be a bird
And turn myself into a full network
To spread the wind of liberation
Everywhere where injustice and exploitation reign,
And to end annihilation and despair
And replace them by light in hope.

CHAPTER 54

Fighting for Humanity

We must unite and unionize
In order to tie a chain of unity for humanity
In the fight against selfishness and resentment
That can tear and choke our hearts.

Oh nature! you who surround us,
Would you like to offer us your assistance?
You constitute our ineffaceable image.
Be our ideal guide, which is irreplaceable.

Life is just a flash of lightning,
Which both obscures and enlightens us.
But, if we can't take advantage of it,
It is already the asphyxiation of our humanity.

The fight for humanity needs to take place hand in hand
In order to prove that we, as a people, are really human.
Fighting for humanity is the real meaning of existence,
Indeed, it is fighting for a better world for all.

CHAPTER 55

Dark Night in the Heart of a Coup

Here comes the night,
Freedom of the Night Knights.
For those who are going to return to their castle,
There are all kinds of cakes.
But for the others in their tiny homes,
There is nothing but a crumb.

Almost everyone is deprived of a breeze,
Because, it is the dog, the cat that enjoy the waft,
And even cross the barrier
From any house and from any border
To find what life has in store for them,
And this, after a lot of maneuvering.

In affluent neighborhoods, there is absolute silence.
Being already at the top, the privileged sleep like a dormouse.
For this category of people, it is the perfect law.
But being at the bottom, the poor experience insomnia,
Which results from all ills and from all sanity.

Every bird and every tree stop singing,
Because it's time for ferocity
Shining under the spark of the stars,
Not to say bullets.
We don't know if life will be reborn
Because everything starts to disappear.

CHAPTER 56

The Danger of Words

So as not to remain silent
We sometimes say what we think.
From there come words and discourses
Often causing so much pain.

Words are the weapon of all human beings.
We emit them, but we rarely measure them.
Words, source of disappointment and frustration,
Can be the basis of all destruction.

The world, they say, depends on the power of speech.
But, doesn't that sound weird, funny?
For some, words are the secret of the heart.
For others, it is the source of all resentment.

The master orator who sometimes behaves as a dictator,
As he pretends to be the great doctor,
Uses words in a grotesque manner
But only to realize later that their violence on others have failed them.

Very often considered as self-defense:
The power of speech, in a certain sense,
Is used to coax the innocent,
And put them in a bloodbath.

Sometimes tinted with all colors,
Speech is synonymous with pain and sweetness.
Sweetness, for those who know how to use it,
And pain to those who have abused it.

CHAPTER 57

You Are My Redemption

With a magical smile, an incredible sense of humor,
You gently and deeply touch the greatest part of my heart.
Knowing you, I feel that I am not an empty heart anymore.
Needless to say, you now own the key to my fragile soul.

Unquestionably, you are physically beautiful in striking ways.
However, internally, your beauty is incredibly incomparable.
The internal qualities you possess make you, without a doubt,
A unique woman transcending this chaotic, confusing world.

Meeting you has helped me develop a renewed vision of the word.
Indeed, you have played an active role in the revolution of my mind,
Particularly, in my new way of observing and connecting with people.
To you, this might sound strange, even silly, but it is my truth.

Getting to know you has made me disregard, even forget:
All my past skepticism and doubt and fear about the future.
And this great feeling incredibly gets stronger and stronger,
Every day, in my open vein, heart, blood, and soul.

Being magically my unique and unique inspiration,
I wish I could be given an opportunity, or simply a chance
Yes, simply a chance to contribute to your happiness.
And the way your heart deserves to receive it.

It is often said that one is only young once in one's life time.
However, together, I feel like that our youth will never fade away.
We'll remain young since our love for each other is eternal.
We are soulmate beyond our last breath on this physical earth.

CHAPTER 58

Dear White Americans
An Open Letter

Let me first acknowledge that I am a privileged Black man. Specifically, I am a tenured professor teaching at a prestigious institution espousing the Jesuit noble tradition. However, at the same time, unlike many of you, I have been subjected to systemic discrimination because of my race. You have white privileges, of which many of you have historically taken advantage to advance academically, professionally, economically, and politically—something those from a different race might not have had the opportunity to do.

Many of you have taken for granted privileges that come with your whiteness. This may be due to the fact that since childhood you have been taught that people of your race have to be on the dominant aisle. This mentality has been reinforced by your former president, Donald Trump, with his slogan *Make America Great Again*, although it is unclear how and why a country, like the United States, needs to be great since it already is. Perhaps the former president meant to say that he wanted to make this country greater for his blind followers.

His ideology is not completely off because the United States has been an empire for over a century, and White Americans, namely White males, have historically been in powerful positions, including political positions like being US president, until the presidency of the former biracial president, Barack Obama. Indeed, many of you, namely White males, have monopolized the political power structure for centuries. Recently, due to the women's movement, we have witnessed a shift in the gender paradigm: some women in both the United States and developing countries have had access to political power. But how many of them have been able to have access to this type of power? Certainly not enough numerically to create a balance in the political machine that has been male dominated.

A shift needs to take place in the political system for both gender equality and equity purposes. For example, despite great achievements made by people of color, including women of color, White male scientists and inventors are mostly noted and praised in our history books. I understand the root cause of some White men's tendency to think in a white male fashion: most textbooks and other important texts, such as the *Holy Bible, the Universal Declaration of Human Rights*, and the *US constitution* were mostly written by men, particularly White males, and their values have consequently been echoed throughout these documents. It is no wonder the content of these texts reflects their biases; they do not represent the voices of all people occupying *the land of the free*—a phrase many people, including politicians, have often used in their speeches to convince of others about their national pride about this country, among other things.

The socio-historical construction of Whiteness is dominantly represented everywhere: in the media, through textbooks, Hollywood movies, the Senate, the Congress, the managerial board of major corporations, in higher education, and in the government. In short, Whites have witnessed the visibility of their whiteness everywhere. Needless to say, whiteness is pervasive in the United States of America, and travels around the world.

White Americans, it must feel good to see people of your race in charge when you turn on your TV set and when you are at work. Does it not? I am sure it does. However, if it feels good to you, what about those who might not be as racially privileged as you? Did you ever wonder how they might feel about not being represented at all or poorly represented in the media and elsewhere? Have you ever thought of that?

Many of you have never had to think about these questions above because of your white privileges. Typical answers from some of you to the questions above tend to be: "It is not my fault I am White." Or "I did not create my white privilege, so why should I feel guilty about it?" Or "Why can't they just be happy with what they have?"

Yes, indeed, no White individual has created his, her or their white privilege. Likewise, people of color did not create their underprivileges due to their skin color. What is more, women did not create their gender oppression. Finally, queer people did not create homophobia or transphobia. They were born different as we all were. However, with some level of awareness, you can reshape and even reinvent the white world you came into; that is, you can use the power attributed to your whiteness to shake up the structure of this world that has given you so many unearned privileges that many of you have taken for granted.

Please remain assured that I am not trying to make you feel guilty about your white privileges. Perhaps, you should feel angry, not with yourself, but with the system that has allowed you to have access to so many resources for merely being White. Many who were born black or brown do not have access to sufficient resources to fulfill their potential. In fact, many have been discriminated in this country because of their race, ethnicity, and religion, like Muslim Americans.

Is this the country you want to continue to live in and expect your children and grandchildren to live in as well? I encourage you to ask yourself this question when you wake up in the morning before having your coffee at Starbucks.

I also encourage you to reflect on the following question before you go to bed: What should I do with my white privileges?

I do not want to dictate to you what to do. I would, however, suggest that you think seriously about using these privileges that have enabled you to accomplish so much in life to serve those of a different race and ethnicity that have been discriminated against in your land. I know it might be too much to ask of you. But please be mindful of the fact that the resources and privileges to which you have had access were already in place waiting for you before you came to this earth. Therefore, you should pay forward as a way to show that you are recognizant of such privileges. In fact, all privileged groups should do the same in order to help the world become a better place for everyone, not only a few.

Because of structural racism, from their birth until their death, White people would most likely have more access to resources than people of color. You can reverse this grotesque social inequity by making a conscious choice to use the same resources and privileges that the socially constructed white race has afforded you to challenge oppressive systems, like systemic racism alongside voucher capitalism, which have historically marginalized people of color.

White Americans, some of you might not know enough about the effects of systemic racism on people of color, as your schools and churches have failed to tell you about them. It is not surprising to me that neither your teachers nor your pastors have shared with you that racism works hand in hand with other systems, such as capitalism and patriarchy, to allow men to keep women in subaltern positions, and racist Whites to racially discriminate against people of color, including immigrants of color.

If you happen to be one of these Whites noted above, you should not feel guilty. The school system that you have been attending since first grade has surely mis-educated you. The Sunday church that you have been attending since you were a child may have concealed the truth from you. Likewise, your family may not have told you what is happening outside your house because they, too, have been victims of the same ignorance with which they have fed you. Finally, your supervisor and co-workers might be as uninformed as you are because the white mainstream corporate media has polluted their mind with massive lies.

As for those who have dared question their whiteness along with their maleness reaching some level of consciousness, it is time to act, particularly if such consciousness has enabled you to realize that you have been lied to about white superiority complex and everything men are expected to do in order to feed the white patriarchal system. Like countless other people, you might not have been quite informed about the source of your white male privileges.

Perhaps, you used to think, and still continue to think, that it was the inalienable right of the White man to monopolize world resources and dominate the global community.

White American fellows, I take the liberty to write this letter hoping that it will help stir up your dormant conscience that has been taken hostage by a racist and patriarchal system run by oligarchs working for the interests of the elite. I am fully aware that we are all part of this system. However, this does not mean that we can't use our strong fists to fight against it. We need to unveil hidden divisive ideology, which this system has used to gain our consent and submissiveness so that we will not challenge the unspeakable, miserable, and oppressive economic, social, educational, sexual, and political situations people of different race, sexuality, and gender have faced in the United States of America and the rest of the world.

Some of you are teachers, professors, journalists, doctors, lawyers, social workers, nurses, pastors, reverends, police officers, or simple employees at both public and private institutions. As such, you're dealing frequently with people from all walks of life. The questions for White teachers particularly beg: How can you educate White students to become conscious and politically aware of their white privileges? How would you steadfastly challenge the system that puts your race on top of a pedestal while subjugating other races? You serve students that have been labeled "inferior" and "stupid" because of their race. Hence, how would you insure that in your class White students and students of color get along and respect one another?

White Americans, it is high time you critically reflect on the biased legal system that has allowed many Whites, particularly White males, to hold most key political and administrative positions in society, whereas other people, including women, people of color, particularly Blacks, Latinxs, Native Americans, and Asians, are massively incarcerated and being murdered nearly daily in the unjust hands of White police officers and civilians. Likewise, poor kids of color are forced to attend unfunded schools and are being taught by poorly trained teachers. At these schools, school police officers routinely arrest them and send them to prisons for minor behavior offenses. Many are from poor neighborhoods plagued with liquor stores, junk food, and drugs on almost each corner ravaged by violence. What do you say about these inequities?

I want to humbly invite conservative White Americans particularly to join in the fight against institutional racism and voucher capitalism that have kept racialized people in socio-economic and educational agonies. Until we realize that we have more to gain by working together to combat human sufferings, we will all continue one way or the other to be victimized by structural oppression that privileges a minority over a majority. And that is not what we want to see continuing to happen in our society and the rest of the world. Hence, I urge you to consider committing to helping eradicate systemic racial, gender, and socio-economic oppression, particularly those of you elected officials and politicians who are in a position to help enact policies aiming to accomplish such a goal.

Author's Note

This letter aims to encourage White Americans, particularly conservative Whites, to take a stance against institutionalized racism so that, collectively as a people, we can co-create a path for the renaissance of a different United States America free of systemic racial, gender, and socio-economic oppression, among others.

AFTERWORD

A Long and Immense Cry That Rips the Air!

Gina Thésée

A long cry, which spreads over an infinite expanse, shrill and deafening, tears the air! The cry of Pierre Orelus, is it a cry of pain, a cry of fear? Is it a cry of anger, a cry of despair? Is it a cry of tears, a cry of sadness? Is it a cry of revolt, a cry of catharsis? Is it a cry of liberation, a cry of emancipation? His cry is all of these at the same time.

I finished reading his book *How It Feels to Be Black in the USA* with a feeling of suffocation…surely echoing Georges Floyd's last cry "I Can't Breathe!" occurred while Pierre Orelus was writing this book. Images of tricontinental trafficking, plantations, slavery, persecutions, black bodies streaked by whipping, the raping of black women, public lynchings…accompany those of the video of the live murder of Georges Floyd on May 25, 2020. When it comes to the "White supremacist" or the "Alright" or murderous police, the shadow of the Ku Klux Klan looms large.

The Ku Klux Klan (KKK) no longer as a group of racists but as an entire society, an entire "ku-klux-klanized" society, where ordinary systemic racism goes hand in hand with democracy. The KKK no longer as a marginal "White supremacist" ideology but as a "ku-klux-klanized" planetary culture where danger is everywhere and omnipresent for "Black and Brown people." The KKK, no longer as cruel individuals, with a criminal mind, who have lost their humanity, but as a "ku-klux-klanisation" of the heart with the share of inhumanity that everyone carries within themselves, whether they be passers-by in a park, suspicious neighbours, police officers, politicians or other social actors in other social spheres or other institutions such as justice, hospital, school, university.

The 59 poetic stories that make up the book parade like a string of wounds that lead us to stop at each station, as for a Christ way of the cross. To the question he asks in the title of his book *How It Feels to Be Black in the USA*, Pierre Orelus outlines for us his answer: to be Black in the United States of America, and also elsewhere in the world, is to be a person always in danger and everywhere in danger, a person who suffocates under the leaden screed of oppression and violence, a person with multiple wounds to his entire Being. Thus, my immersion in his book allowed me to detect:

- Bodily injury to the physical body of Blacks: "In Search of a Safe Place" (Chapter 2); "From the Ghetto to the Ivory Tower" (Chapter 4); "Vetted Immigrants" (Chapter 9); "The COVID-19 Pandemic of Color" (Chapter 23); "Cancer Sucks" (Chapter 26); "Bloody Day" (Chapter 46).
- Emotional Wounds in Black Hearts: "Feeling the Blues" (Chapter 1); "The Oppressed of the Americas" (Chapter 6); "Phobias in the United States" (Chapter 10); "Why Are Black People So Angry?" (Chapter 12); "When Love Is Gone" (Chapter 28); "Involuntary Exile" (Chapter 44).
- Intellectual Wounds within the thought of Blacks: "Feeling in Exile in My Own Land" (Chapter 7); "The Misrepresentation of People of the Global Majority" (Chapter 8); "What Happens to the Black Nation" (Chapter 13); "In Memory of George Floyd" (Chapter 17); "The Day of Revolt" (Chapter 45); "Life as a Circle" (Chapter 52); "I Have Another Dream" (Chapter 54); "The Danger of Words" (Chapter 58).
- Spiritual Wounds to Black Souls: "The Depressed" (Chapter 33); "Death of a Nation" (Chapter 27); "Fear of Death" (Chapter 29); "Where Is the God for Black People?" (Chapter 40); "God, Where Are You?" (Chapter 47).

Yet, despite everything, along the way, beams of iridescent light began to pierce and spring: "We're Rising up in Multi Colors" (Chapter 19); "On Forgiveness" (Chapter 35); "Living in the Future" (Chapter 36); "The Beauty in Solitude" (Chapter 38); "Only the Truth Will Set US Free" (Chapter 43); "Light in Hope" (Chapter 55); "Fighting for Humanity" (Chapter 56).

Also, a certain resistance-resilience seems possible thanks, in particular, to the female figure and the children: "The Resilient Black Woman" (Chapter 5); "The Woman Who Floats" (Chapter 15); "How Real Love Feels Like?" (Chapter 22); "You're a Beautiful Wave" (Chapter 31); "On Co-Parenting" (Chapter 32); "Dear Black Women" (Chapter 49); "African Goddess" (Chapter 51); "Black Youth" (Chapter 53). The poetic story "The Woman Who Floats" (Chapter 15) is particularly touching. It reads like an ode in homage to the Woman, a feminine figure who brings together the qualities of "Mother-Earth," with a loving, attentive, benevolent, and caring spirit:

> She is a mother, wife, daughter, sister, lawyer, niece, senator, secretary of state, learner, artist, student, state representative, dancer, writer, athlete, entrepreneur, nurse, journalist, nurse aid, housekeeper, administrator, poet and a teacher who never stops reinventing herself. She is a mother who lovingly gives and genuinely cares for all children. A strong woman who chooses hope over despair, who survives miscarriages and cancer. A

woman who loves music and likes to shake her buddy; a woman with a big smile and soul.

Transcending wounds, a form of spiritual healing, seems possible through the celebration of one's "Blackness": "Black Pride" (Chapter 14); "I Am Black and I Am Enough" (Chapter 21); "Discovering African Spirituality" (Chapter 34); "Honoring Our Black Ancestors" (Chapter 37); "Black Exodus" (Chapter 41); "Open Letter to Our Ancestors" (Chapter 42).

The poetic story "When Love Is Gone" (Chapter 28) is particularly questioning. It is read in two registers at the same time. The first register is that of the intimate sphere, a love story has ended, that between two people. The second register of reading concerns the collective sphere; this time, a love story between two communities, the white community and the black community, a love story that died without ever having existed.

Similarly, the poetic narrative "You're a Beautiful Wave" (Chapter 31) can be read simultaneously in the registers of the intimate, the social and the ecological. Indeed, what is the nature of this "Beautiful Wave"? Is it a person whose meeting brings love back to life? Or a social current that restores hope for a possible reconciliation between racial communities? Or, a humanist wave coming from Nature itself, "Mother-Earth," which alone can save the suffering soul: "Your human wave keeps coming, and shines people's souls and spirit. You're not only a wave but also the fountain from which stems the spring water your loved ones, among others, drink daily, and from which you're inspiring hope for many, known and unknown."

The last poetic account of the book is an open letter, "Dear White Americans: An Open Letter." In his endnote on this subject, Pierre Orelus indicates:

> This letter aims to encourage White Americans, particularly conservative Whites, to take a stance against institutionalized racism so that, collectively as a people, we can co-create a path for the renaissance of a different United States America free of systemic racial, gender, and socio-economic oppression, among others.

Like an outstretched hand, despite everything, in search of Truth, Reparation and Reconciliation, Pierre Orelus outlines a kind of critical pedagogy intended for the followers of racial oppression and the institutions that make it their structure. Slowly, patiently and eloquently, he demonstrates, illustrates, explains systemic racism and the resulting social pathologies "for Black and Brown people," from the cradle to the grave, in the environment, housing, work, consumption, health, education, politics, media, future. He invites, urges, even begs "Dear White Americans" to recognize that:

> we have more to gain by working together to combat human sufferings, [...] I urge you to consider committing to helping eradicate systemic racial, gender, and socio-economic oppression, particularly those of you elected officials and politicians who are in a position to help enact policies aiming to accomplish such a goal.

Like Awad Ibrahim, who wrote the foreword to the book, I celebrate the "strong poetry" of Pierre Orelus in his book *How It Feels to Be Black in the USA*. In doing so, I celebrate the absolute poet that is Pierre Orelus who, between the essay and the pamphlet, between literature and orality, between English and French, knew how to put into dialogue his pain and his fear, his anger and his despair, his revolt and his catharsis as a Black man, while making them dance with his urgent dreams, his hopes, his struggles, his educational utopia and his radical love of humanity.

Ou Est le Dieu Pour le Peuple Noir?

Pere de l'univers, bref Dieu.
Puisqu'on t'appelle Dieu.
Rien moins qu'un individu
Pensant que ce devoir lui est du
Pour te parler. Me voici.
Tout seul, je suis ici
Dans une piecette de maison
M'inspirant pourtant la raison
Pour te questionner, non pas t'interpeller,
Et pour savoir si tu t'amuses a somnoler,
Car beaucoup de personnes
Restent a sonner des claxones
Pour s'assurer si tu les entends,
Car elles ne veulent pas perdre le temps
Dans une croyance insensee
Qui les rend maintenant lasse.
Moi, pour ne pas perdre la foi,
S'il te plait, communique moi les vraies lois,

Lois de justice, de sagesse, et de lumiere
Apres quoi, je ferai de bonnes prieres.
Ne voulant pas te nommer monsieur,
Et pour etre sur si que t'es aux cieux,
Dis-moi, si t'es une fille ou un garcon
Pour que j'accomplisse ma mission.
Je marche sur beaucoup de religions
Professant leur foi aux differentes regions.
Ne sachant pas ce qu'elles font,
Je ne puis decouvrir leurs trefonds.
Oui. Dieu: le pere, le fils et le saint esprit
Mais, moi je suis completement pris
De ces mots qui me paraissent inexplicables
Et que nul ne peut rendre justifiables.
Mon cher, ou que tu sois
Vetu d'un manteau ou d'une robe de soie,
Soit blanche, rouge, jaune, soit noire
Tronant dans un chateau ou dans un couloir,
Je te prie de m'expliquer ces mots
Qui me causent tant de maux.
On les a certes explique dans la bible.
Mais, ils me paraissent incomprehensibles.
Es-tu reellement notre guide?
Alors, pourquoi tout nous est rigide?
Si tu existes, donne-nous le secret de la vie
Dont nous avons grandement envie
Es-tu le vent, la poussiere ou l'air?
Pourquoi pas une lueur de ta lumiere?
Alors, devrais-je croire au vent
Qui me tracasse tres souvent?
Dois-je croire en un etre supreme
Ne sachant pas s'il me regarde meme?
Devrais-je me jetter dans l'aventure
Tout en ignorant les lois de la nature?
Pere de l'univers, bref Dieu
Puisqu'on t'appelle Dieu.
Si franchement tu me veux
Tiens-moi ce grand voeu:
Projette-moi ta lumiere.

Pauvrete Noire

Pourquoi la faim, bref la misere
Nous obligent de gagner la mer
Sans nourriture, sans aucune destination,
Et, pourtant, on est d'une nation?

Pourquoi tous ces mots: le chomage
Qui nous met tres souvent en rage?
Pourquoi la caste, le racisme, l'inegalite,
Corollaires de la pauvrete et la ferocite?

Pourquoi ne peut-on pas sourire?
Pourquoi souffrir et meme mourir?
Mourir, par qui? Par Dieu ou la nature?
Ou par de la ferocite d' une dictature?

Pour quoi la mechancete, la tuerie
Qui se faisant sous un pilori?
Pourquoi l'aristocratie, la burocratie?
Pourquoi ne pas faire grandir la democratie?

Pourquoi l'evangile de la resignation
Voulant nous faire garder la soumission?
Pourquoi l' univers nous tourne la face?
N'y avons nous pas aussi une juste place?

Si le messie nous a cree avec purete et gout,
Alors, pourquoi veut-on nous jetter dans l'egout?
Enfin pouquoi l'individualisme, l'egoisme?
Pourquoi pas l'humanitarisme.

Pourquoi, oui pourquoi la pauvrete
S'il existe, le partage, et la fraternite?
Partager dans l'est de fraternite n'etant que des mots
Qui enduisent les gens en des raisonnement faux.

Maintenant, d'ou viennent la pauvrete et la misere
Qui muent les hommes, les tiers-mondistes, en here
Sous ce ciel bleu hypocrite et grimacant
Ou tout semble immonde, corrompu et menacant?

Pourquoi naitre dans la puanteur de la pauvrete,
Et puis grandir et trepasser dans la mendicite?
Est-ce le voeu de la nature ou du ciel?
Ou l'inique partage terrestre du miel?

La pauvrete, n'est-elle pas le resultat
Ou que ce soit, dans n'importe quel Etat
De la jouissance d'un enfant bien allaite
Au prejudice de sa mere maltraitree?

Oh! a n'en pas douter:ce sont les yeux qui voient
Des rapaces masques utilisant toute sorte de voix,
Gagnant la franchise, l'ame des innocents
En vue de sucer la quintessence de leur sang.

Ancetres Africains

Bien chers les trepasses,
Vous qui aviez, certes, passe,
courageusement, de vie a trepas
En essayant de briser beaucoup de remparts.
Maintenant sur cette vieille terre,
Il n'y a que l'injustice et la misere.
Peut-etre, durant votre epoque, jadis,
Vous y aviez goute le miel du paradis.
Quant a nous, heritiers de cette terre
Qui nous trouvons a cette nouvelle ere,
Nous ne connaissons, sous ce grimacant ciel,
Que la nausee, la repugnance et le fiel.
La nourriture terrestre etant impartageable,
Pour nous: c'est la miette. O nature charitable!
Ainsi, que nous faut-il entreprendre?
Pour que cela puisse cesser et suspendre.
On nous dit chaque jour attendre et prier
Amerement, nous essayons meme de crier.
Mais helas! nos cris ne parviennent au sommet
Ou se trouvent, peut-etre, Dieu ou Mahomet.
Alors, chers ancetres, qu'elle est la bonne voie
A prendre, si nous voulons que notre voie
Soit partout resonnee, entendue

Pour reclamer ce qui nous est du?
On se trouve entre l'enclume et le marteau.
Donc, il nous faut necessairement votre manteau
Afin de nous proteger contre le vent de l'egoisme
Nous empechant de pratiquer l'altruisme.

I Discours Sur La Verite
Sur le chemin de la verite,
Parseme d'obstacles et d'obscurite,
Ne se trouve t-il pas une lueur d'espoir
Qui puisse constituer notre miroir?

La verite qui sort du fond de l'ame
Blesse, certes. Mais c'est une excellente arme.
La verite devrait est une boussole de tout etre,
Meme quand on peut en souffrir peut-etre.

Oh comme il est infame de se nourrir du mensonge,
Qui depersonnifie, obscurcit, falsifie et ronge!
La verite, purete de la conscience,
Devrait etre la quintescence
De tout homme, de tout individu.
Car, elle lui est humainement due.

Pourqoui craindre dire ouvertement la verite
Quand il est question de transformer l'humanite?
Car, la ou verite est pronee, la lumiere est jaillie,
Partout, dans n'importe quel region ou pays.

La verite, c'est l'aurore du printemps.
Elle est jeune, et ce, en tout temps.
Etant reference ideale pour tout chanbardement,
Elle juge tout un chacun equitablement.

L'homme libre, c'est l'homme veridique.
Mais, il doit etre aussi scientifique.
Car, s'adonner, s'orienter vers la science,
C'est deja liberer son esprit, sa conscience.

Pour journalistes, avocats veridiques, credibles,
La verite peut rendre leur tache facile, possible.

Sans ignorer qu'ils peuvent en souffrir
Et peuvent meme en devenir matyrs.

La verite est parfois fielleuse et mielleuse.
Mielleuse parcequ'elle rend la vie lumineuse.
Fielleuse, parcequ'elle demasque l'hypocrisie
Et, par la suite, provoque la haine, l'heresie.

Pour eviter une vie pleine de mensonge et de tenebre
Il faut dire la verite, surtout si on veut repandre la lumiere.
Fut-ce au prix de sa vie or de son existence.
Qui peut etre sujette a la souffrance.

Exiles Involontaires

O infame exil involontaire
Bien souvent sur sa propre terre!
EXILE est exclu de toutes les ambiances sociales
Comme si on n'etait pas natif, natal!

Exiler a la maniere des necessiteux, des immigres
Quittant parfois leur pays a l'encontre de leur gre
Pour aller trimer dans une terre etrangere!
Oh c'est vraiment les consequences de la misere!

Combien la vie de ces proscrits egorges,
Trimant a tout heure a l' etranger
Pour aider, epauler leurs proches natals
Est sujette a la nostalgie et est fatale!

Souvent, c'est le hasard d'un voyage maritime,
Dependant du caprice d'un ocean de crime,
Crime provenant des bateaux animalises
Visant a rendre ceux qui sont a bord paralyses.

Ils partent, ces exiles, sans idee de retour
Pour cesser d'etre des damnes, des vautours.
Meme quand ils manquent leur parents et amis,
Ils ne peuvent rien faire, car la vie leur est ennemi.

Misere, diable noire, o sacrilege, infame!
Parmi ces sacrifies, se trouvent meme des femmes
Vendant leur force productive, fragile de travail
A l' etranger, aux exploiteurs sans entrailles.

Exiles involontaires, leur vie est mutilee.
Perplexes, aigris, ils n'osent meme parler,
Car leur coeur est gonfle de nostalgie et haine
Resultant de frustration, humiliation et peine.

Chasses par la misere de leur propre pays
A la recherche d'un lieu où l'eau vitale a jailli,
Le jour pour eux est la nuit et la nuit est le jour.
Ils sont prive meme du temps pour dire bonjour.

Il semble que la nature ne leur appartient,
Car parfois ce sont meme des chretiens
Qui prient et les autres jouissent de leurs prieres
Croyant naivement que les riches sont pour l'enfer.

O les forces de la nature, roi de l' univers!
Ces mots qui sont construits, eriges en vers
Sont destines a les encourager, les reconforter,
Ces exiles involontaires, ces maltraites.

Si on prone que la vie est l'union, le partage.
Alors, pourquoi, oui pourquoi une telle vie sauvage,
Menee par les fils, les enfants de la terre
Dans une contree soit disant etrangere?

Haiti, 7 Fevrier 1986

Jour de sang, de reviviscence.
Partout, ce peuple reclame,
A tout son esprit, son ame,
La fin de toute manigance.

En tout lieu, c'etait un jour de "boukman."
Les lions se comportaient en gentleman

Pour s'echapper du rouleau compresseur
Concu justement pour les oppresseurs.

En 7 Fevrie 86 le soleil Haitian avait sourit
A tous, jadis, privant du mais, du riz
Sur cette terre, selon la vieille adage,
Où il n'existait pas de juste partage.

Tous ceux accablant par la peine
Avaient repris brusquement haleine,
Grace a ce doux et cet oasis vent.
Vent de la liberte ne soufflait auparavant.

Mais helas! 7 fevrier 1986. Oui 7 fevrier!
A tourne sa face aux ouvriers,
Constituant le pilier d'haiti Thomas
Qui se trouvent maintenant dans le coma.

Haiti, 29 Novembre 1987

Ce jour la, tout le monde etait content
Et croyait meme qu'il etait temps
Pour aller jetter un bulletin
Vers huit, neuf heures du matin
A la recherche d'une verite
Pour le bien-etre d'une societe.

Oui, c'etait a la ruelle "Vaillant"
Où des hommes braves, vaillants,
Imbus du courage, du patriotisme,
Allaient prouver leur heroisme
Tout en liberant leur esprit et leur ame
Que des sanguinaires en achetaient a coup d'armes.

Le Miserable

Pourquoi vivre si sa vie est le chagrin?
Sans amour, isole comme de petits grins,

Situes au milieu d'une foret,
La où il n'ya aucun rai.

Pourquoi son existence
Si tout lui est souffrance?
Frustrer, souffrir de toute envie,
Sur quoi alors reposerait sa survie?

Reflechissant, il ne voit qu'a cette nouvelle ere
L'argent represente le seul maitre.
Ne voulant pas se compromettre,
Alors que devrait-il faire? Se jetter en mer?

La vie, ou es-tu?
Il risque d'etre foutu.
Dieu! prouve-lui ton omnipotence
Qu'il attend avec impatience.

Vivre sans jamais connaitre un jour de miel,
Car, chaque jour c'est la deception, le fiel.
Non. La vie, elle ne le merite pas.
Non. Il doit passer de vie a trepas.

Enfant pauvre, toi qui representes pour ce monde l'avenir,
Pourquoi veut-on partout te trahir?
Ton regard nous fait penser a la misere;
Comment n'es-tu pas issu aussi d'une mere?
Croupir dans la misere, c'est toi qui le veut?
Non, ce ne serait jamais ton voeux.

Desormais! la vie, ce mot doit etre tabou,
Si pour vivre, on doit se vautrer dans la boue.
Pouquoui ce proverbe: chacun a une etoile.
Pourquoi, te loges-tu a la belle a l'etoile?
Comment est la tienne exclue de cet aster?.
Alors pour toi, tout est fini et contraste?

Fruit de ce monde! c'est ta peau qui te hait.
Pourquoi cette contraintre: faire la haie
Dans une rue ou le fatras est le seul maitre,

Et qui risque inevitablement de tout compromettre.
Quel sera donc le jour de ta liberation, ta delivrance?
Puisque pour toi, presque chaque jour c'est la souffrance?

Pourquoi veut-on que tu te nourrisses de miettes?
Comment te considere t-on comme un muet ou une muette?
Aie de patience, on attend le grondement de cet orage
Pour enfin briser cette pyramide d'exploitation
Axant sur l'hypocrisie, le mensonge et la corruption.

Femme Noire

O femme!
Notre ame,
Sans toi
Nulle joie.

Vraie deesse
De toute caresse,
Ton existence
Est notre quintessence.

Source de poesie,
Tu stimules notre frenesie
D'une maniere folle, sans fin.
Avec tes suaves mains.

Parfois mechante, tres mechante,
Mais toujours charmante
Avec son coeur,
Clef du bonheur.

Serve de la jeunesse
Sans tes caresses !
N'a pas de sens
Quoi qu'on pense.

Vraie reference
De preference

Pour les poetes
Des autres planetes

O femme!
Notre ame
Sans toi
Nulle joie.

Meme quand rusee,
On ne peut oser
Vivre sans elle
Car, c'est notre zele.

Infidele, insincere,
Pourtant, on la venere.
Quel dilemme !
Quel probleme !

Que l'on soit misogyne,
On est son origine.
Alors que faire ?
Peut-on en defaire ?

Homme, femme.
Vie, ame.
Voila ineluctable
Et indubitable!

Les hommes bestiaux la saccagent
Quand ils s'enragent.
Pourtant sa compassion and douceur
Remedient a toute haine et douleur.

Black Woman

Toi, ce n'est plus pareil.
Mon coeur, mon ame et mon oreille,
En ecoutant ta voix d'ange et de noblesse,
Atteindent le point culminant d'allegresse.

Toi, avec ton sourire d'adolescence, jovial
Tu me fais penser, certes, a la brise matinale
Qui inspire aux jeunes ecrivains et poetes
Les idees les plus claires et nettes.

Toi, pour qui j'eprouve mes plus tendres sentiments
Tu me pousses a me demander sincerement
Est-ce que tu n'es pas la quintessence
De tout mon etre et mon existence.

Toi, qui merites d'etre contemplee et adoree
Devrais certainement, malgre vent et mare,
Etre la jouisseuse d'un ocean d'amour pur
Remplit de fleurs printanieres et parure.

Toi enfin, qui pourras combler tous mes vides.
J'espere que pour moi ton coeur ne soit pas rigide
Afin que je puisse etre le principal acteur
Dans le theatre de ta vie et ton coeur.

      Parure de l'univers
      Je t'offre ces vers
      En recompense
      A ton importance.

La complexite de la vie

Voici l'aube et le lever du soleil.
Bientot va etre le coucher du soleil
Ici tristesse, la bas melodie.
Etant inhumain, c'est une parfaite comedie.
Mais, conscient, c'est le battement vif du coeur
Resultant du depit, de la repugnance et la rancoeur

Aujourd'hui: c'est la joie et la douceur.
Alors que demain ne peut-etre que malheur.
Voici le soleil. Il est tres ardent.
Tout le monde en est sur les dents.
On marche, on mange et on est content.
Or ce n'est que pour un laps de temps.

La vie n'est d'autre qu'un jeu
Qui peut mettre parfois tout en jeu.
Et, si on cherche a la definir
On peut meme en souffrir.
Entretemps, le seul roi nous attends: la mort,
Qui provoque de la peine, des cris et remords.

La Jeunesse

Que represente ce mot
Puisqu'elle souffre presque de tous maux.
Apparamment sans guide et sans miroir
Pourtant, elle est l'avenir et l'espoir
Du monde, y compris cette societe.

Oui, la jeunesse n'est pas innocente.
C'est pouquoi elle devient impatiente
Pour une liberte qu'elle reclame,
La où elle se trouve a toute ame
Par l' esprit de solidarite.

Travail et liberte, synonymes de la vie,
S'en priver, sur quoi reposerait sa survie?
Elle souffre, parlant de justice, et democratie
En depit de toute frustration et peripetie.

Eh bien, la vie, c'est souffrir et mourir!
Non. Il reste un chemin a parcourir.
Chemin où tous les jeunes vont concerter
Pour l'octroi de dignite humaine, justice et liberte.

Je voudrais

Je voudrais parler, m'exprimer
Pour exorter les opprimes
A se liberer de ce joug d'esclavage
Que les exploiteurs en font l'usage
Pour s'approvisioner et s'enrichir.

Je voudrais
Je voudrais etre le coeur des laisses-pour-compte
Qui ne se rendent peut-etre meme pas compte
De leur misere, de leur vie inhumaine,
Et qui pourtant se precipitent de dire"amen"
Apres des preches ne visant meme pas a les affranchir.

Je voudrais
Je voudrais m'arranger au cote des moutons
Pour les dire d'abandonner ce vieux ton,
Le ton de la docilite, de la naivete
Pour qu'ils cessent d'etre exploites.

Je voudrais
Je voudrais etre le messager de Dieu
Sans le dessein de m'eriger en dieu
Afin de precher la parole de la vie, de la liberation
Sans etre teintee d'aucune couleur de la resignation.

Je voudrais
Je voudrais que la haine, la famine et l'injustice
Cedent le pas a l'amour, le mieux-etre, la justice
Pour que la mort infantile, la mechancete
Cessent de se produire dans la cite.

Je voudrais
Je voudrais que les grands oiseaux: l'autriche, l'aigle
Cessent de planer sur les petits pour violer leur regle
Que leurs ancetres ont si dignement etabli
Et qui ne doivent etre jamais plonge dans l'oubli.

Je voudrais
Je voudrais concretiser, caresser
Sans arriere pensee, sans lasser
Les reves des ouvriers, des paysans
Souffrant depuis bien des ans.

Je voudrais
Je voudrais enfin etre un oiseau
Et me muer en un plein reseau

Pour repandre le vent de la liberation
Partout ou regnent l'injustice, l'exploitation
Pour aboutir a l'aneantissement du desespoir
Tout en regnant la lumiere et l'espoir.

Lutter pour L'humanite

On doit s'humaniser et lutter
Pour nouer une chaine d'unite
Afin de combattre l'egoisme et la rancoeur
Qui peuvent dechirer et etouffer nos coeurs   .

Oh la nature! toi qui nous entoures
Voudrais-tu nous offrir ton concours?
Car tu constitues notre image ineffacable
Voire notre guide ideal, irremplacable.

La vie n'est qu'un coup d'eclairs,
Qui nous obscurcit et nous eclaire.
Mais, si on ne peut en profiter
C'est deja l'asphyxie de l'humanite

Lutter pour l'humanite main dans la main
Afin de prouver qu'on est vraiment humain.
Lutter pour L'humanite constitue le sens,
Laboratoire de la vie et de l'existence

Nuit Sombre au Coeur d'un Coup d'Etat

Voici l'arrivee de la nuit,
Liberte des chevaliers de nuit.
Pour ceux qui vont regagner leur chateau,
Il y a toute sorte de gateaux.
Mais, les autres dans leur maisonnettes,
Il n'y a rien sinon que miette

Presque tout le monde est prive de brise,
Car, c'est le chien, le chat qui brisent,
Et meme franchissent la barriere

De toute maison, de toute frontiere
Pour trouver ce que la vie leur reserve
Et ceci, apres beacoup de manoeuvres.

En haut, c'est le silence absolu.
En bas, ce qui ne peut pas etre resolu.
Etant deja au cime, on dort comme un loir.
Pour cette categorie, c'est la parfaite loi.
Mais, se trouvant au centre, c'est l'insomnie,
Resultant de tous maux, de toute sanie.

Tout oiseau, tout arbre cessent de chanter,
Car, c'est l'heure de la ferocite
Faisant sous l'etincelle des etoiles
Pour ne pas dire des balles.
On ne sait pas si la vie va renaitre.
Car, tout commence a disparaitre.

Le Danger de La Parole

Pour ne pas garder le silence
On dit parfois ce qu'on pense.
De la viennent la parole, le mot
Causant bien souvent tant de maux.

Parole, c'est l'arme de tout etre.
On l'emet, mais on ne la penetre.
Fruit parfois de deception, de frustration,
Elle se trouve a la base de toute destruction.

Le monde, dit-on, depends du pouvoir de la parole.
Mais, cela ne resonne t-il pas bizarre, drole?
Pour certains, la parole est le secret du coeur.
Pour d'autres, elle est le friut de toute rancoeur.

La clef maitresse de tout orateur-dictateur,
Qui veulent se faire passer pour le grand docteur
Des mots et meme des idees cauchemartesques,
Utilisent la parole parfois d'une maniere grotesque.

Tres souvent consideree comme l'autodefense:
Le pouvoir de la parole, dans un certain sens,
Est utilise pour amadouer les innocents.
Et leur faire plonger dans un bain de sang.

Enfin, teintee certaines fois de toutes couleurs.
La parole, elle est synonyme de douleur, de douceur.
Douceur, pour ceux qui savent l'utiliser,
Et douleur a ceux ell cause de la nausee.

www.ingramcontent.com/pod-product-compliance
Lightning Source LLC
Chambersburg PA
CBHW051528230426
43668CB00012B/1781